# Knit Green

# Knit Green

## 20 Projects & Ideas for Sustainability

JOANNE SEIFF

WILEY

Wiley Publishing, Inc.

# Credits

**Acquisitions Editor**
Roxane Cerda

**Development Editor**
Natasha Graf

**Production Editor**
Donna Wright

**Technical Editor**
Deborah Robson

**Editorial Manager**
Christina Stambaugh

**Publisher**
Cindy Kitchel

**Vice President and
Executive Publisher**
Kathy Nebenhaus

**Interior Design**
Erin Zeltner

**Project Photography**
Megan Wynn

**Graphics**
Laura Campbell
Brooke Graczyk
Melissa K. Smith

For general information on our other products and services or to obtain technical support please contact our Customer Care Department within the U.S. at (877) 762-2974, outside the U.S. at (317) 572-3993 or fax (317) 572-4002.

Wiley also publishes its books in a variety of electronic formats. Some content that appears in print may not be available in electronic books. For more information about Wiley products, please visit our web site at www.wiley.com.

Library of Congress Cataloging-in-Publication Data:
Seiff, Joanne, 1973–
  Knit green : 20 projects and ideas for sustainability / Joanne Seiff.
     p. cm.
  ISBN-13: 978-0-470-42679-1
  ISBN-10: 0-470-42679-9
  1. Knitting. 2. Sustainable living. I. Title.
  TT825.S44 2009
  746.43'2—dc22
                              2009020173

Printed in the United States of America

10  9  8  7  6  5  4  3  2  1

Book production by Wiley Publishing, Inc., Composition Services

# Dedication

*For Paul and Carol Brouha, my best friend's parents, who introduced me to conservation, buying locally, and thinking and talking about environmentalism long before it was common to do so.*

*Also, for Anne Brouha, my best friend, who keeps me thinking about these (and many other issues) and finally, for Jeff Marcus, my biologist husband, who mentors and supports me when it comes to sustainability.*

# Acknowledgments

Many thanks to the yarn companies who donated yarns: Mango Moon Yarns, Connie Taylor of Bayeta Gordo, Green Mountain Spinnery, Knit Picks, Lion Brand Company, Crystal Palace Yarns, and Lorna's Laces.

Even more thanks to my sample knitters, Judy Seiff (thanks, Mom!) and Bonnie McCullagh, whose fine work helped to support my designs. I couldn't have knit it all without you!

Thanks to my fabulous publisher, Wiley, and the wise editors who have kindly made this book what it is: Roxane Cerda, Natasha Graf, Donna Wright, and tech editor, Deborah Robson. Jodi Bratch, photo person extraordinaire, helped choose many good images for this book. Megan Wynn, of Megan W Photography, did a beautiful job of shooting the photos for the knitting designs. Thanks also to all the models, who looked so lovely as they posed!

I've learned a great deal over the years from environmentalists, biologists, and conservationists of all stripes. If you're one of the folks who talked to me at my husband's university biology department events, thanks for educating me! Universities have been working toward sustainability for quite a while, and I benefited from that informal part of my undergraduate education at Cornell University. *Knit Green's* ideas also owe much to the farmers, chefs, and foodies who paved the way first, helping us to think about our food, where it comes from, and how we eat it.

Finally, to you, dear readers, thanks in advance. It's you who will reshape the spectrum of "green" knitting goods available in the future, through your careful purchases and requests at your local yarn shops and your creative new businesses. A special thanks also goes to those who work to maintain environmentally friendly fiber farms now and in the years to come.

# Table of Contents

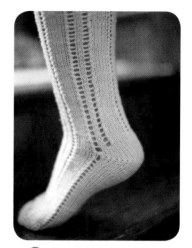

# Introduction

Psst. Let me let you in on a secret. I'm a moderate. I want to support environmental sustainability, but guess what? I haven't gone off the grid, given up industrially made clothing, or sold my car. Instead, I've committed to small changes in my life. These changes are things I can maintain on a day-to-day basis. Some of the changes mentioned in this book in regard to knitting may initially appear conflicting. How can you "Buy Local" in your town *and* support a far away women's co-op that produces yarn in a developing country? Well, on the surface, many of the options I present here may appear to be in opposition with one another. However, these different possibilities may instead be complementary suggestions.

**Never doubt that a small group of thoughtful committed citizens can change the world. Indeed, it's the only thing that ever has.**

—Margaret Mead

We have quite a bit of disposable income in the industrialized world, and I'm going to bet you're a lot like me. Perhaps you spend a fair amount of your cash on your yarn/fiber/fabric stash? What if those purchases were all spent thoughtfully, on yarn that supported your underlying values? What if some of your choices involved using what you had instead of buying everything you wanted? All of these ideas can make a difference in knitting *and* limiting one's environmental impact. This book will explain how, but its scope is limited. No one book can solve all these issues, but it may get us started thinking about how to do more.

It's popular right now to fill up environmental literature with statistics on one's carbon footprint or carbon neutral living. As you might expect, the statistics regarding the environmental impact of knitting yarns are not quite cutting edge. Instead of filling up your head with numbers that are hard to back up, I've chosen a different approach. I've looked at today's numbers quoted in the general media and offered you some guidelines without the statistics. Beside the fact that the yarn statistics might not have been readily available, I also think the numbers are all changing very quickly. Folks are catching on to living in a more "green" way. In 5 years, I believe many of these numbers will have changed…and I hope, in my most optimistic moments, that the statistics will have improved.

You may already know I'm a knitwear designer, a spinner, and a freelance writer. I've also tried to be environmentally conscious for a long time…as I suspect we all need to if we hope to make a difference in preserving our planet. I happen to be married to a biology professor, so I've heard my share of the sustainability discussions around our dining room table, at parties, and at other events. I even took a year of college-level biology and earned the worst grade of my college career! However, that's exactly the kind of person to write a book on this topic. I hope the result is easy to read, understandable, and best of all, offers you suggestions for how to make a big difference while still enjoying knitting.

Each of the following chapters introduces you to issues that relate to the environment, sustainability, and concerns that are often linked to these topics. The designs that follow the chapters have a connection to the essays and sidebars, and are created to take you a step beyond simply reading the book. Every design indicates both a yarn that you might choose to knit with and information about how to substitute another yarn. Make your own choices about what you want to knit, whether it's local, organic, vegan, fair trade, sustainably farmed, or another issue altogether. I hope this book helps you on your knitting journey toward making a difference…one stitch at a time!

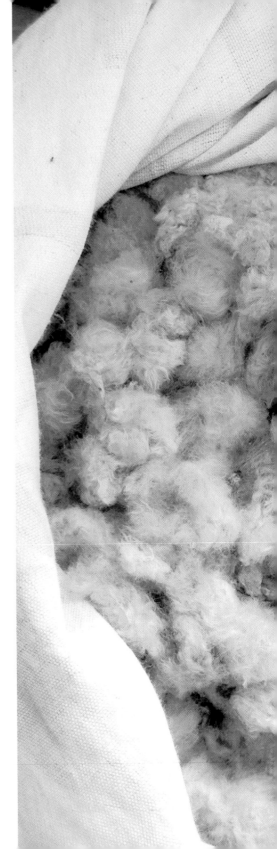

Supporting
Biodiversity

Imagine if everything we knitted was the same. Same boring color, same texture, same weight…knitting would lose some of its charm, wouldn't it? Yet, maintaining all of these different kinds of fibers, yarn weights, colors, and types of yarn isn't always going to be a sure thing. In order to be certain there is always a rich choice at the yarn shop, we need to think about where those yarns originate. Once you're knitting with a fabulous new wool, cashmere, or linen yarn, you'll agree. We can't afford to lose any biodiversity on our planet!

∞

*The American Heritage Dictionary of the English Language* (Fourth Edition) defines biodiversity as, "The variability among living organisms on the earth, including the variability within and between species and within and between ecosystems." Although terms like *biodiversity* or *ecological diversity* sound complicated and may seem a little far from knitting and sustainability, these concepts tie into our yarn (fiber) supply, whether it's derived from animals, plants, or man-made processes. In this chapter I give three examples of popular fibers and how we can support biodiversity. Many of these ideas apply to all fibers, so don't hesitate to ask questions when buying any kind of knitting yarn.

## Wool: A Yarn from an Animal

I'll start with an easy example. Many of our fibers come from animals' wool, fiber, or hair. Sheep offer a great diversity of wool from thousands of different kinds of sheep breeds such as Merino, Karakul, or Shetland. Where do all those breeds come from?

People domesticated sheep thousands of years ago for their wool, milk, and meat. The farmers who bred those sheep chose particular attributes which worked well in their geographic areas. In some cases, the sheep evolved into breeds without human intervention. Sheep that have been selectively bred by people or by their environment tolerate heat and cold differently, resist different kinds of diseases, have differing rates of success when lambing, and produce vastly different kinds of wool. Those different kinds of wool are an important example of a benefit to humans from biodiversity. Merino produce soft, fine wool that is ideal for babies or clothing worn next to the skin, but it doesn't wear as well as a slightly coarser wool, like Shetland. By contrast, coarse wool from Karakul sheep is made into many of the carpets that have lasted for generations underneath our feet—but is too itchy to wear next to the skin. Different breeds of sheep are around for important ecological reasons and *diverse* functions.

*Natural green-colored cotton, once rare, is making a comeback.*

As our farming grew more industrialized and global, our breeding did as well. No longer are farmers in one area of the world breeding sheep entirely on their own. Geographic pockets of certain breeds of sheep don't remain isolated and cut off from other parts of the world as before. Sometimes this is good as we can strengthen one breed by cross-breeding with another. However, if we want to maintain some of these fascinating breeds of sheep, we must help support and maintain their existence.

One way to do this is by financial support. Purchase yarn from farmers who raise these rare animals. While it may seem counterintuitive, if you eat meat, consider buying lamb for dinner from those farmers as well. (Freezer lamb exists because 50 percent of lambs born are male, and a farm only needs a ram or two around. Rams can be dangerous to handle, so farmers try to reduce risk to people and other animals in this way.) If consumers demonstrate a demand, farmers will raise more diverse breeds of sheep and these rare breeds will no longer be endangered.

If you live in an urban area and don't bump into any farmers, don't despair! Many companies work on biodiversity, but a well-known one, Rowan yarn, now produces a British Sheep Breeds line of yarns that use a variety of heritage breeds. If you prefer to support a small farm, many of them are on the Web, and you can even find local wool and yarn at this Web site: www.localharvest.org.

▶ *Once in danger of extinction, the Navajo-Churro sheep is the oldest heritage sheep breed in the U.S.*

How can a knitter find out what breeds need to be supported? Check out the American Livestock Breeds Conservancy in the United States or the Rare Breeds Survival Trust in Britain for more information. Many countries have equivalent rare breed protection efforts. These organizations offer all sorts of information about supporting and maintaining rare breeds of farm animals.

## Cotton: A Plant Fiber

When it comes to maintaining our planet's biodiversity, wool is just one example! In fact, globally, far more cotton is used than wool. Therefore, cotton should also be part of a biodiversity solution. Although cotton historically grew in a variety of colors, modern cotton fields are full of snow white bolls. What happened?

Five thousand years ago, native people in South America, Africa, and Asia cultivated natural-colored cottons. These cottons were short stapled (the fibers were short), which required skilled spinners and weavers to process the cotton into usable textiles. Over time, longer stapled white cottons became dominant. These were especially useful when spinning and weaving were no longer done by hand. Industrialization in the colonial period required longer stapled fibers for use in the cotton gin (which removes cotton seeds from the boll by machine), mechanized spinning jenny, or looms.

For a time, white cotton ruled not only in the field but also in legislation. James M. Vreeland

Jr. writes in the 1999 *Scientific American* that in 1931, "the Peruvian government had issued a series of laws and decrees aimed at destroying perennial, pigmented forms of native cotton in an effort to protect the all-white varieties that were commercially viable…. Pesticides were liberally applied, and the long-standing, successful tradition of crop rotation was abandoned." A great amount of genetic diversity in cotton (the diversity that enables a variety of colors to exist) was lost during this period. However, despite the dominance of white, long stapled cotton, individual farmers bucked authority and grew colored varieties of cotton in some areas of the world, including Peru, and even Acadian hand spinners in the Mississippi Delta region of the United States. In the Soviet Union during World War II, dyes weren't available, so colored cottons were grown and served as a substitute. At the time, natural-colored cotton wasn't considered commercially viable in the United States.

Today, it's pretty easy to find naturally green cotton jeans in the department stores or organic beige, brown and green yarns in your local yarn shop. How did these long lost varieties of cotton become available again commercially?

In the 1990s, natural-colored cottons became popular again because of increased concerns about pesticides, dye usage, and pollution. This was only possible because of people like James Vreeland, who helped to establish the Native Cotton Project in Peru where colored cottons are again farmed on a larger scale, and Sally Fox, who worked to develop and breed longer stapled colored cottons in the United States. These efforts to maintain the genetic diversity of cotton also reduce pesticide usage, because some older strains are more resistant to pests and disease than conventional cotton. In a sense, every natural-colored cotton yarn or textile helps to reinforce not just the future biodiversity of cotton, but the biodiversity of the ecosystems that are seriously harmed by pesticides dumped into the environment through conventional cotton farming. You can start by buying natural-colored organic cotton yarns. These are widely available, from Lion Brand and Bernat as well as Pakucho (James Vreeland works with this company), Sally Fox's Foxfibre, Rowan, and many other yarn companies.

## Hemp: An Underused Plant Fiber

What about a useful fiber that doesn't require any pesticides and is easy to grow organically? Hemp is an ancient bast fiber, like flax (linen) that is grown all over the world. It tolerates a lot of different soil types, stabilizes the soil, and even draws excess chemical nitrogen from over-fertilized soil, which prevents it from polluting waterways. It feeds lots of wildlife with its seeds…and has the potential to reduce human famines with its high amounts of protein. Hemp produces a fiber that is available now as a great knitting yarn.

The downside to hemp is its relationship to cannabis (marijuana). The United States outlawed the growing of hemp in 1970 even though it has no possibility of causing drug addictions, as its relative, cannabis, does. In fact, the United States historically grew hemp, but is now the only country who outlaws it as a crop. In this situation, supporting the use of hemp can also be a vote for supporting wildlife biodiversity. Buying hemp yarns can be an opportunity to "vote" for hemp. In no way does a vote for hemp support drug use; fiber-producing hemp can't get anyone high except for knitters, who love the yarn it produces! Some companies producing hemp yarns include Hemp for Knitting, EnviroTextiles LLC, Hemp Traders, and The House of Hemp.

If you can't get your hands on hemp yarns, consider linen or ramie yarns as a substitute. The yarn qualities are much the same: hard-wearing and strong plant fibers. You'll be helping to maintain plant fibers used for textiles for thousands of years.

Supporting our planet's biodiversity for knitters means we should support, maintain and discover the miraculous fiber capabilities on our planet. From sheep breeds to hemp to cotton varieties, we have enormous natural opportunities when it comes to fiber. If we want to keep all those varieties around, we must sustain the farmers who support older and heirloom varieties, as well as taking care to choose rare and diverse fibers.

# Hemp Placemats

Hemp is the ideal fiber for table linens because it's hardwearing, machine washable, and crisp. Many placemats available in stores can't be washed, which seems entirely counter-productive, given their purpose on the dining table. Beyond practicality, these placemats have style, too. Choose two bright colors that coordinate with your décor or rely on a single color and let the stitch pattern's texture shine through. Ideal for all sorts of entertaining, these placemats might look especially nice with glass dishes in particular. Bon appétit!

## Skill Level
Easy

## Size
One size
Pattern makes 4 placemats

## Finished Measurements
12" × 17" (30.5cm × 43.2cm)

## Materials
- Color A: 2 skeins of Lanaknits Designs Hemp for Knitting allhemp6 yarn, 100 percent Hemp, 165 yd. (150m), 3½ oz. (100g), color 027 Aubergine
- Color B: 2 skeins of Lanaknits Designs Hemp for Knitting allhemp6 yarn, 100 percent Hemp, 165 yd. (150m), 3½ oz. (100g), color 019 Sprout

or

- 330 yd. (300m) each of any 2 colors of machine washable DK weight yarn with the appropriate gauge

or

- 660 yd. (600m) of any 1 color of machine washable DK weight yarn with the appropriate gauge
- U.S. size 5 (3.75mm) straight or circular needle, *or size to obtain gauge*
- Row counter
- Tapestry needle
- Blocking pins

## Gauge
18 sts and 25 rows = 4" (10cm) over Placemat patt rep

## Pattern Stitches

### Placemat Pattern

Worked over a multiple of 4 sts.

With Color A:

**Row 1 (WS):** *P2, k2, rep from
* to last 4 sts, p2, k1, wyif
sl1 pwise.

**Rows 2 (RS) and 3 (WS):** Work
as for Row 1.

**Row 4 (RS):** *K2, (yo, k2, pass
yo 2 sts),* rep from *.

**Rows 5, 6, 7:** Work as for
Rows 1–3 above.

Change to Color B:

**Row 8 (RS):** Knit.

**Row 9 (WS):** Work ribbing opposite to
Color A, as follows:

*K2, P2, rep from * to last 4 sts, k2,
p1, wyif sl1 pwise.

**Rows 10 (RS) and 11 (WS):** *K2, p2, rep
from * to last 4 sts, k2, wyif sl1 pwise.

**Row 12 (RS):** K2, *k2, (yo, k2, pass yo
2 sts),* rep between * to last 2 sts, k2.

**Rows 13, 14, 15:** Work as for Rows 9–11
above.

**Rows 16–22:** With B, work St st (knit 1 row,
purl 1 row).

Change to Color A:

**Rows 23–30:** Work St st, beg with purl row.

## Instructions

**note** When switching colors, cut yarn, leaving
tail at the end of a row. At the beginning of a
row where you have left a tail, work in ends as
you knit, twisting the tail with the working yarn
behind stitches on WS as you go.

## Make Four

CO 56 sts.

Work Placemat Patt Rows 1–30 three times.

Work Placemat Patt Rows 1–15 one time.

BO.

## Finishing

Weave in ends, if necessary. Wet block by
dampening placemat. Pin flat to dry.

17" (43.2cm)

12" (30.5cm)

Zafu: A Churro Cushion

# Zafu: A Churro Cushion

A zafu is a thick, round meditation cushion, ideal for sitting on the floor. This Asian-inspired cushion is ideal for your couch, for use as an ottoman, or for additional seating. Hardwearing Navajo-Churro rug yarn works well if you'd like a cushion that lasts. Purchasing this rug yarn helps maintain the Navajo-Churro sheep, king of the Southwest rug tradition and a rare breed sheep. Knit in the round, you build this cushion as you go and choose how tall to make it, how to stuff it, and even the perfect buttons. At last, knitting as interior decoration that also helps promote sustainability!

## Skill Level

Easy

## Size

One size

## Finished Measurements

Diameter: 15" (38cm)

Height: 6½" (16.5cm)

Roughly 47" (119.4cm) in circumference

## Materials

- 2 skeins of Bayeta Gordo yarn, 100 percent Navajo-Churro Rug Weight Wool, 400 yd. (366m), 16 oz. (454g), color Sand

or

- 800 yd. (732m) of any rug weight or bulky yarn with the appropriate gauge
- U.S. size 11 (8mm) double-pointed needles
- U.S. size 11 (8mm) circular needle, 40" (102cm) long, or size to obtain gauge
- 7 stitch markers
- Tapestry needle
- 9" (23cm) matching zipper
- Stuffing (see note): Wool batting or roving, eco-friendly fiber fill, or Organic Cotton stuffing
- Sewing needle and matching thread
- 2 buttons, 1" (25mm) diameter

**note** Zafu cushions are traditionally stuffed with buckwheat or kapok. I have suggested using natural fibers or recycled fibers for stuffing this cushion. (See chapter 4 for more information about environmentally friendly stuffing options.) Other options include cutting up old T-shirts and other rags to use as stuffing for this cushion. If you should choose to use buckwheat or kapok, it might be necessary to create a liner inside of the knitting to keep the stuffing from poking through the knitted fabric.

## Gauge

10 sts and 12 rows = 4" (10cm) with 2 strands of yarn in stockinette stitch

## Pattern Stitches

### Fabric Stitch

Worked over an odd number of sts.

**Rnd 1:** *K1, sl1 wyif, rep from * to last st, k1.

**Rnd 2:** K1, *k1, sl1 wyif, rep from *.

Rep rnds 1 and 2.

# Instructions

## Cushion Bottom

Using 2 strands of yarn, CO 6 sts on 1 dpn. Kf&b in each st, for a total of 12 sts.

Distribute the sts evenly on 3 dpns. There will be 4 sts on each needle. Join and pm. (Clipping a safety pin or open-ring marker into the fabric may be the easiest way to mark this beg of rnd.)

**Rnds 1–4:** Knit around working kf&b in last st at the end of each needle; at the end of rnd 4 there will be a total of 24 sts.

**Rnd 5:** *K3, kf&b in next st, pm, K3, kf&b in last st at the end of the needle,* rep 2 more times.

Continue knitting in the round, always kf&b in last st before marker and in last st at the end of the needle.

When sts become too crowded on dpns, change to circular needle, adding 3 markers to mark the inc points previously at the ends of the dpns.

Continue increasing in the same fashion until there are 120 sts, with 20 sts in each section between markers.

At beg of next rnd, inc 1 st for a total of 121.

Knit 1 rnd even, removing all markers but the first, which marks the beg of the rnd.

## Cushion Sides

Work Fabric Stitch patt. When Fabric Stitch section measures 5½" (14cm), work zipper opening as follows:

## Zipper Opening

At beg of next rnd, BO 24 sts. Work the rest of the rnd in Fabric St.

At beg of next rnd, CO 24 sts. Work the rest of the rnd in Fabric Stitch patt, as established.

Work 3 more rnds in Fabric Stitch patt.

## Stitch-In Zipper

With zipper closed and RS of ½ of zipper facing RS of 1 edge of opening on cushion, using matching sewing thread and needle, attach zipper with a running st to that side of the zipper opening (see Figure 1). Unzip the zipper to st the other half of the zipper along the second edge of the opening—RS to RS (see Figure 2). Reinforce the zipper by doing a second seam with whip st on the WS. Tuck the zipper ends to the inside of the opening and tack them down (see Figure 3).

## Cushion Edge

Continue working in Fabric Stitch patt until cushion side measures 6½" (16.5cm) or desired height.

At beg of next rnd, dec 1 st for a total of 120. Knit 1 rnd even.

## Cushion Top

At marker, sl1, k1, psso, k19. *Pm, sl1, k1, psso, k18, rep from * to end of rnd.

Continue knitting in round, always slipping 1, k1, psso after marker.

Change to working with dpns when there are too few sts to work comfortably on the circular needle.

When your hand will still fit comfortably through the cushion top, stop knitting and stuff cushion (adjustments can also be made through the zipper.).

Continue knitting and decreasing as above, until 1 st is left in each section (total of 6 sts), removing markers on this rnd.

**Next Rnd:** *Sl1, k1, psso, around (3 sts rem).

**Next Rnd:** Sl1, k1, psso, k1 (2 sts rem).

**Next Rnd:** Sl1, k1, psso (1 st remains). BO last st.

## Finishing

With tapestry needle and 1 strand of matching yarn, close up CO edge in Cushion Bottom.

Weave in ends.

Dampen or spray with water to block.

Shape cushion while damp to make the shape you'd like; add additional stuffing through zipper opening if necessary. Allow cushion to dry; it will hold shape.

With matching thread and needle, sew on buttons to cover the CO and BO and to add a slight dimple to the cushion's center.

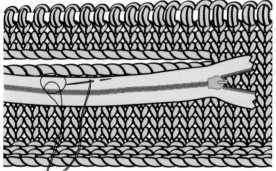

Figure 1

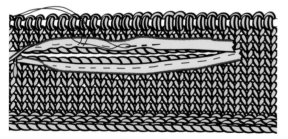

Figure 2

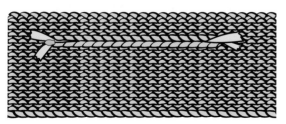

Figure 3

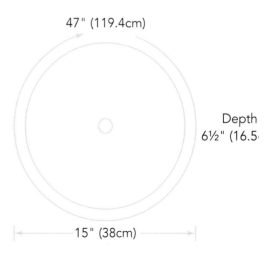

47" (119.4cm)

Depth 6½" (16.5

15" (38cm)

# Sustainable
# Farming Practice

Years ago, I visited a farm that helped me see what farm sustainability might be like. On a sunny spring day, my husband and I visited an Ontario sheep farm. The owner gave us a tour herself. The sheep were crossbred to produce exactly the kind of long wool she liked to spin. Every sheep had a name, and all their wool was handspun by the owner and a few other spinners. In the farm's shop, the beautiful hand-knit sweaters and hand-woven pieces were hard to resist. Every garment had a handwritten tag that explained which sheep, spinners, knitters, or weavers contributed to its production. The farm's working border collies guarded the shop as well, as if to say "this wool is from our sheep, too!" At this one farm, the whole sustainable process, from the shepherd to the value-added product (those amazing sweaters), was on display. It was a fascinating glimpse into what farm sustainability might have been once, and could be again.

❧

So, what *is* sustainability? Farming sustainably means several things. The issues usually mentioned are the farm, the farmer, the community, and land stewardship. These issues work hand in hand: the farm and farmer must be adequately sustained. That means the farm must be economically prosperous and fertile enough to feed and maintain the farm animals, the farmer, and the farm family.

For instance, this is no small thing when considering the small amounts earned for wool. Each farm family has a different budget for these issues; many families have one partner who works off the farm to bring in income, while the other partner raises the fiber, as well as gardens or animals that feed the family. Yet, there's a fundamental disconnect for most of us when it comes to understanding farm life. Have you ever asked kids from the city where milk comes from? "The grocery store, of course!" they will answer with a big grin. I've even heard the follow up, "Where does chocolate milk come from?" "Brown cows." This anecdote, or something similar, is often recounted by people in the slow food movement, farmers, or just those who bemoan how disconnected we are from the earth.

The sad truth is that the average yarn shop *is* also often disconnected from where the fiber comes from. Yarn shops usually buy their stock from a sales representative, and that person connects with a distributor, and…eventually the boxes filled with yarn for our future sweaters arrive. So, how many knitters ask, "Where does our yarn or fiber come from?"

If it's a naturally grown fiber, (which, unlike oil-based polyesters, can be maintained sustainably)

*Yaks eat only about one-third the amount of hay or grass as a commercial cow and don't require a finishing ration, eliminating the need for steroids and hormones. They need no special fencing and are inherently disease-resistant and cold-hardy, making them an ideal candidate for sustainable farming. These yaks are residents of the Bijou Basin Ranch in Colorado.*

it came from farms. Things like wool, alpaca, Angora, silk, cashmere, yak, cotton, hemp, flax, and ramie all were likely raised on a farm, or by a shepherd or farmer. Farmers and shepherds carry a heavy burden when it comes to being a good steward of both animals and the land. In order to make a living, they must produce large and beautiful quantities of fiber for sale. When they sell their fiber, they are likely to make a very small amount, perhaps not even enough to cover their costs, never mind a profit, unless they sell directly to a consumer. For instance, sheep farmers who sell fleeces to the commercial wool pool in their region may earn less than $1 a pound for their raw wool. When washed, carded and spun, that might be equivalent to an 8 ounce skein of yarn. By the time you're purchasing the yarn at the knitting store, you're paying the farmer, the woolen mill, the yarn designer, the distributor, the sales representative and the yarn shop owner for your knitting pleasure.

Farming communities are often left out of the equation, but are crucial to the notion of sustainability. Farmers need adequate infrastructure in order to sell their crops at a fair price. They also need basic necessities such as medical care, grocery stores, banks, and schools. Rural communities need to provide these things within a reasonable distance so farmers can reach their closest community without driving a long way, which is costly in terms of time and fuel.

Also, not all farms are in rural areas. Farms that exist outside of cities in what once were rural villages are often being encroached upon by development. Cities (and citizens) must emphasize the need to maintain zoning that allows for farming and to provide positive support for the farmers in their midst. Farming is hard enough; growing

▶ *Some fiber enthusiasts have begun keeping their own sheep, offering a more personal connection to the wool they use and the land on which they live.*

urban areas should not look upon the land and farmers who supply their food, fiber, and other needs as getting in the way of new subdivisions.

## What About Land Stewardship?

Land stewardship is the first thing most people focus on when talking about sustainability. Taking care of the land, enriching, maintaining, and safeguarding the soil, water, air, wildlife, and the people are important issues, too. However, when a farmer's profit margin is so small, many farmers focus almost exclusively on sustaining their families and communities. Sustaining the land comes last in some equations, when from an environmental standpoint, it must be at the forefront if we wish these natural resources to be around for generations to come.

Let's start with safeguarding the soil. Many farming activities draw nutrients as well as water from the soil. Plant fibers such as cotton, flax, or ramie, for instance, grow as other crops do. In a sustainable farming model, these crop fields would be rotated, fertilized with natural composts, and planted with cover crops that helped boost nitrogen and other nutrients back into the soil. However, farmers who are just looking to make

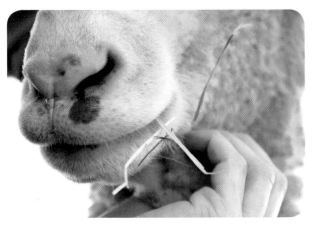

the biggest profit from their land often prefer to avoid these time-consuming and costly steps. They want to grow monoculture crops (one crop) rather than a more sustainable rotation of multiple species. They use large amounts of pesticides and synthetic fertilizers to boost crop production…and this is big business. To the relief of the large chemical companies, it works. The single crop approach continues on farms throughout the world. That single crop manages to grow in worn-out soil.

What about the water? Large scale, single-crop farming, as mentioned, uses large-scale chemicals. Those chemicals often are washed into nearby bodies of water. For instance, the Mississippi River drains about 41 percent of the water in the central United States and dumps into the Gulf of Mexico, and this area has an enormous dead zone caused each year by nitrogen and phosphorus fertilizers. The dead zone lowers the oxygen in the water to the point that many shrimp, fish, snails, crabs, starfish, and other bottom dwellers die there. The affected marine area varies from year to year but is roughly the same size as New Jersey.

What fiber-related crops use the *most* pesticides and fertilizers? Corn (Ingeo) and soybeans (soy silk) use the most, according to the United States Department of Agriculture (more on these fibers in chapter 3). Cotton is next—there's a reason why it's called "King Cotton." In 2003, 4.3 pounds of pesticide were used on every acre of cotton, according to the United States Department of Agriculture (USDA) and in 2000, 142 pounds of synthetic fertilizers were applied to each acre of cotton. While the numbers may differ from harvest to harvest, that's a lot of chemicals—and much of it ends up in our water. What's worse? The Environmental Protection Agency (EPA) concluded in the same time period that 7 out of 15 of the chemicals used were possible, likely, probable, or known human carcinogens.

As anyone who has seen a crop-duster plane knows, the chemicals are often sprayed into the air on top of those fields. Some of the chemicals, if inhaled, are very dangerous. So, our air is affected, too. Finally, as one can imagine, wildlife is vastly affected by this kind of farming. Everything in the ecosystem, from insects to birds, from snakes to mammals and finally humans, can be affected adversely by the soil, water, air, and harvest.

The example I've given is for plant fibers, but damage can also be done to an ecosystem when animals are not carefully monitored. If their fields are overgrazed, the plants that keep the topsoil safe from erosion can be eaten—and the topsoil will be washed away when it rains. Even if an animal hasn't been treated with chemicals, its manure alone can contaminate the water with bacteria if the land's not properly managed. The manure might not decompose safely and when it rains, bacterial run-off could get into a river or stream. In fact, manure alone, and the methane it produces can be a pollutant if it isn't managed responsibly. In New Zealand, where livestock are a major producer of the country's greenhouse gas emissions, they are actually working on an inoculation that will reduce the amount of methane produced by ruminants such as sheep. (This causes only 2 percent of United States' greenhouse gas emissions, but causes more than half of New Zealand's greenhouse gas emissions, according to the British newspaper, *the Telegraph*.)

## Buy Organic Cotton

These scenarios sound gloomy, but there are a lot of opportunities to make change here. The first is an easy economic one. Cotton is the second most frequently used fiber globally, after synthetics. Choose to buy organically raised cotton. If there is a demand for cotton grown without pesticides and synthetic fertilizers, there will be farmers who meet that demand. There is also an intermediary step some farmers take that reduces their chemical usage, and produces "eco-friendly" or "green" cotton…and while this isn't as good as organic methods, every effort counts. While farmers' yield may initially lessen when they choose to go organic or "eco-friendly," there will be an associated reduction in costs (chemicals are expensive) and almost immediately improve the land they farm as well as their health. Avoiding chemical usage and moving toward more sustainable practice can immediately affect the stewardship of the land, the farm, farmer, and community.

## ෨ Peace Silk ෨

You may have recently come across someone advertising "peace silk." What does it mean? Can silk be raised sustainably in this way?

People have cultivated silk for thousands of years. As a result, the process is somewhat standardized. The key to the process is an unpleasant detail, central to the creation of the best silk. Silk is spun by a caterpillar, which becomes a pupa in its cocoon. The cocoon is made of silk, and a silk moth will then make a hole in the cocoon to emerge—as a moth. The moth will leave the cocoon to lay her eggs, and the eggs will hatch as hungry caterpillars and begin the cycle again.

Most silk is produced from *Bombyx mori,* which is actually a cultivated silk. These caterpillars have been bred to produce silk and are maintained and farmed in much the same way that we raise domesticated farm animals like sheep and pigs. Unlike the wild silk moth, the *Bombyx mori* cannot survive without the care and upkeep of humans.

During this process, if the silk is to be reeled off the cocoon without damage, the pupa inside must be killed so it will not make that hole in the cocoon and break the silk filaments. Most pupa are killed quickly with heat, either in a hot oven or by being steamed and boiled. According to Laurie Brooke Adams (known as Mother Mastiff online), "in poverty-stricken areas, the extremely high protein in the silkworm pupae is the highest and best quality protein available to most poor people. Freshly boiled pupae are cheap, and considered a great treat…. Silkworm pupae are literally part of the food chain as well as part of the fiber process, and the most valuable source of cheap protein available to many impoverished folk."

Only a very small number of moths are allowed to hatch from their cocoons, roughly 1 in 300 to 500, according to Adams, a fiber artist who raises her own silk. Although the damaged cocoons called peace silk (also called *Ahimsa,* meaning

## Buy Plant Fibers Like Hemp, Flax, or Ramie

As mentioned in chapter 1, another great fiber to consider buying is hemp. It's a plant that's good for the soil, needs little or no pesticides, and offers the potential for food production as well. Also, hemp is a strong, long wearing fiber that softens as it is used. It lasts a long time, thus reducing wear and tear that would cause someone to need to purchase new clothes more quickly.

"nonviolence") have always existed as a product of the silk industry, it is a byproduct. Deemed inferior because of its short staple length, this small amount of silk was often made into stuffing for duvets, silk hankies for spinners and other products that brought less money when sold. Today, some of this byproduct is being marketed as peace silk and sold for premium prices because of its alleged "nonviolence."

The tail end of this lifecycle also leaves it absolutely clear that sustainability isn't really possible if all or even most silk were raised as Ahimsa or peace silk. When the moths emerge from their cocoons, the female moths will each lay hundreds of eggs. When they hatch, hundreds of caterpillars will need to be fed from each moth that lays eggs. It is impossible to feed the many billions of caterpillars that would result from any sort of large-scale production of peace silk. The deaths that would occur would not, perhaps, be the first pupae in the cocoons, but the hundreds of eggs or small caterpillars that each female moth would produce.

In the end, we might have to view silk in its true context. A sustainable lifecycle for silk production does inherently involve death at some point in its cycle, and it may well involve boiled pupae that feed hungry, impoverished people. An unsustainable system might be one in which many young caterpillars defoliate whole trees but still fail to satiate the caterpillars. The trees die. The caterpillars die slowly of starvation. The ecosystem is unworkable.

People have domesticated the silkworm, just as dogs, cats, sheep, goats, or pigs have been bred over centuries. A sustainable system for these creatures involves human interactions and care. Alas, while this system may include death along the way, it may also be managed carefully, so that animals (even silkworms) live good lives and have quick, humane deaths.

Want to read more about raising silk moths and about peace silk? Check out Michael Cook's Web site, www.wormspit.com. Michael is an incredible spinner and fiber artist who works wonders with caterpillars and silk.

Linen (flax) and ramie are also a good investment if you'd like to purchase a hardwearing fiber that lasts. While you're knitting these fibers, they may feel stiff, but plant fibers soften over time. My best friend's family came to the United States from Belgium, and Belgium's famous linens, that is, bedclothes made from flax, came with them. Sixty some years later, those well worn but beautiful bed "linens" are some of the world's softest and most comfortable sheets for sleeping on. I love sleeping over at their house!

A third option for your pursuit of sustainable fibers might be more exotic. Wild fibers, such as buffalo or yak, can also be grown sustainably. Herd management enables biologists and ranchers to manage and boost these populations while also harvesting fiber. Nettle (also called Aloo) is a plant fiber harvested from the wild by Nepalese women, who take care to leave some to reseed for the next harvest. Yarn companies who sell these fibers should be proud to boast that they are safely harvested. Check their labels and Web sites.

## Buy Carefully Sourced Wool, Mohair, Cashmere, Alpaca, Llama, and Pygora

Wool, mohair, cashmere, alpaca, llama and even Pygora (another goat fiber) can be grown sustainably. Many shepherds adequately maintain and build wildlife habitat and ecosystems while raising sheep, goats, and other livestock. How can you find this kind of yarn? Small farm family businesses that produce their own yarn lines will be happy to tell you how they work toward

sustainability. Other yarn companies may issue statements on their Web sites, or even on their labels, explaining their approach. Many companies these days will not only explain where their wool yarn is from, but who raised it, how they raised it, and even why they processed it the way that they did!

## Buy Locally

One last part of this discussion is the issue of buying local fibers. When one buys locally, there's a chance to observe exactly how the farmer's fields and animals are managed. There's also a reduction in transportation costs from the farm to your knitting basket. Overall, this equation is the best for the environment in terms of one's carbon footprint, as long as the farmer is conscientious about environmental issues.

While this will be covered in another chapter, sometimes one must also ask if buying locally is always the best sustainability practice in your region. For example, Merino sheep are bred with lovely fine wool and many folds in their skin, which help them to grow more wool. Yet in hot, humid climates, these folds can harbor pests that will dangerously harm the animals. Some shepherds in hot, humid regions raise Merinos anyway and use a lot of pesticides to keep them healthy. Others choose sheep that are better adapted to the climate at hand. Sometimes, it may make better sense to support a farm that is sustainably managed in a healthy climate for the particular animal or plant, and then pay the energy costs to have that fiber shipped to you. These are the complicated decisions one must think through—and yes, even a skein of yarn makes a difference. If we're all buying just one skein of yarn…it adds up.

Basketweave Hat

# Basketweave Hat

This is a quick and flexible unisex design. Knit in soft wool, from the crown of the head down, this design can be made for matching adult and kid hats. Want to try luxury instead? The adult hat pictured here is knit in Shokay Yak Down, harvested sustainably in the Himalayan region of China. Help maintain a centuries-old Tibetan herding existence—and wear the softest hat you've ever owned!

## Skill Level

Easy to Intermediate

## Size

Child (Adult)

## Finished Measurements

18 (21)" (45.7[53.3]cm) circumference
7 (8½)" (17.8[21.6]cm) from brim to top of crown

## Materials

### For Child's Hat:

**note** One skein makes two children's hats. Consider knitting one for the intended child and one for charity.

- 1 skein of Sheep Shop Yarn Company Sheep 1 yarn, 100 percent wool, 130 yd. (119m), 3.5 oz. (100g), color F31 Spring Green

or

- 130 yd. (119m) of any Aran/heavy worsted weight yarn with the appropriate gauge

### For Adult's Hat:

- 1 skein Shokay Pure Yak Down Shambala yarn, 100 percent yak, 164 yd. (150m), 3.5 oz. (100g), color Chocolate
- U.S. size 8 (5mm) double-pointed needles
- Row counter
- Stitch marker
- Tapestry needle
- Matching thin sewing elastic (optional, for Adult Hat if knit in Shambala)

## Gauge

### With Sheep 1:

16 sts and 20 rows = 4" (10cm) in both Basketweave patt and stockinette stitch

## With Shambala:

16 sts and 24 rows = 4" (10cm) in Basketweave patt; 18 sts and 26 rows = 4" (10cm) in stockinette stitch

## Instructions

**note** If using Shambala, bear in mind this very warm fiber is not as elastic as wool. It will stretch to accommodate a larger adult's head but won't spring back into shape. See finishing instructions to add elastic for this reason.

**note** Work increases by knitting in the front and back of stitch to create spiral increase hat crown.

## Hat

CO 6 sts and knit, distributing evenly over 3 dpns.

Pm and join, taking care not to twist sts.

**Rnd 1:** Inc 1 in each st for a total of 12 sts.

**Rnd 2 and every even round:** Knit.

**Rnd 3:** *K1, inc 1 in next st, rep from * to end for a total of 18 sts.

**Rnd 5:** *K2, inc 1 in next st, rep from * to end for a total of 24 sts.

**Rnd 7:** *K3, inc 1 in next st, rep from * to end for a total of 30 sts.

**Rnd 9:** *K4, inc 1 in next st, rep from * to end for a total of 36 sts.

**Rnd 11:** *K5, inc 1 in next st, rep from * to end for a total of 42 sts.

**Rnd 13:** *K6, inc 1 in next st, rep from * to end for a total of 48 sts.

**Rnd 15:** *K7, inc 1 in next st, rep from * to end for a total of 54 sts.

**Rnd 17:** *K8, inc 1 in next st, rep from * to end for a total of 60 sts.

**Rnd 19:** *K9, inc 1 in next st, rep from * to end for a total of 66 sts.

**Rnd 21:** *K10, inc 1 in next st, rep from * to end for a total of 72 sts.

## For Adult Hat Only:

Continue as above, increasing each odd round, until there are a total of 84 sts.

Work St st until hat measures 6" (15.3cm). Work Basketweave patt as follows.

## For Both Sizes:

Work Basketweave brim:

**Rnds 1–5:** *K2, p2, rep from *.

**Rnds 6–10:** *P2, k2, rep from *.

**Rnds 11–15:** *K2, p2, rep from *.

**Rnd 16:** BO in patt.

## Finishing

Weave in ends. With a tapestry needle and CO tail, sew up hole at the top of the hat.

Block hat.

If using Shambala, you may want to run a thin strand of elastic through sts on the WS of hat brim. Yak down is not as elastic as wool and will not cling to the ears as effectively. To do this, use a tapestry needle and work a running stitch in the last rep of the basketweave brim on the WS of the hat to create greater elasticity.

Basic Bermuda Bag

# Basic Bermuda Bag

Retro bags are always in style! While this pattern is designed to fit a new Bermuda bag that is available for sale online (check the Resources section in the Appendix), an intermediate level knitter will likely be able to adjust the pattern size if necessary. Whether you find a Bermuda bag at your local thrift shop or purchase a new handmade one, this is a clever way to knit a bag (cover) for every outfit! After your initial investment of the Bermuda bag, consider making yourself covers to match a variety of outfits. Using small amounts of organic cotton, locally grown wool, or other natural fiber options can help keep your project sustainable as well as fashionable, but any worsted weight yarn from your stash that knits at the appropriate gauge is a good option.

## Skill Level
Easy

## Size
One size fits the Jesse B. Collection Bermuda bag as specified below.

## Finished Measurements
Oblong measuring approximately 9½" (24.1cm) wide × 8½" (21.6cm) long

## Materials
- Color A: 2 skeins of Lion Brand Organic Cotton yarn, 100 percent Organic Cotton, 82 yd. (75m), 1¾ oz. (50g), color 004 Cypress
- Color B: 1 skein of Lion Brand Organic Cotton yarn, 100 percent Organic Cotton, 82 yd. (75m), 1¾ oz. (50g), color 001 Vanilla

or

- Color A: 164 yd. (150m) of any worsted weight yarn with the appropriate gauge
- Color B: 82 yd. (75m) of any worsted weight yarn with the appropriate gauge
- U.S. size 6 (4mm) straight or circular needles, *or size to obtain gauge*
- U.S. size 6 (4mm) double-pointed needles, *or size to obtain gauge*
- Row counter
- Tapestry needle
- Safety pins (optional)
- The Jesse B. Collection Bermuda Bag

**note** This pattern is designed to fit the Jesse B. Collection Bermuda Bag. This bag is manufactured in Pennsylvania and available in the United States. There are a wide variety of other similar bags available for sale and in thrift stores. While these bags will be a reasonable substitute, their measurements may vary. Acquire and examine your bag before casting on and adjust sizing and buttonhole placements accordingly.

## Gauge

18 sts and 26 rows = 4" (10cm) in stockinette stitch

20 sts and 36 rows = 4" (10cm) in seed stitch

## Pattern Stitches

### Seed Stitch

Worked over an even number of sts.

**Row 1 (RS):** *K1, p1; rep from * across.

**Row 2:** Knit the purl sts and purl the knit sts.

Rep row 2 for seed st.

## Instructions

**note** For firm edges, wherever possible at the end of each row, wyif, sl1 pwise.

### Bag Cover Side (Make Two)

With Color A and #6 (4mm) straight or circular needles, CO 18 sts.

**WS:** Purl 1 row.

Working in St st (knit 1 row, purl 1 row), inc 1 st at beg and end of every row 7 times until there are 32 sts on the needle.

Work 1 row straight without increasing.

## Make First Buttonhole

**RS:** K2, BO 2, knit until last st, wyif, sl1 pwise.

**WS:** P28, CO 2, p1, wyif, sl1 pwise.

**Next row (RS):** Inc 1 st at beg and end of row—34 sts.

Work 5 rows of St st.

## Buttonhole #2

**RS:** *K2. BO 2, knit until last st, wyif, sl1 pwise.

**WS:** P30. CO 2, p1, wyif, sl1 pwise.

Work 6 rows St st.*

## Buttonhole #3

Rep between ** above 1 more time to form Buttonhole #3.

## Buttonhole #4

**RS:** *K2. BO 2, knit until last st, wyif, sl1 pwise.

**WS:** P30. CO 2, p1, wyif, sl1 pwise.

Work 5 rows St st.

**Next Row:** Dec 1 st at each end of row.

## Buttonhole #5

**RS:** *K2. BO 2, knit until last st, wyif, sl1 pwise.

**WS:** P28. CO 2, p1, wyif, sl1 pwise.

**Next row:** Knit 1 row without decreasing.

Dec 1 st at each end of row, every row, until there are 18 sts on the needle.

Work 1 row even.

BO.

Wet block both sides of cover by washing or dampening at this point. Block these before adding I-cord edging as described below.

## Seed Stitch Strip

With Color B and #6 (4mm) straights or circular needles, CO 10 sts.

Work Seed Stitch patt as described above.

When piece measures 20" (50.8cm), BO.

## Create Attached I-Cord Edging

**note** The following technique will join the pieces and create a piping-style edging at the same time. If preferred, one can knit the I-cord separately and sew the parts together afterward.

With 2 #6 (4mm) dpns and Color B yarn, CO 2 sts.

Line up seed st strip with the left side of one Bermuda bag cover with RS up and buttonholes closest to you.

Measure 1" (2.5cm) from last button hole (see the figure on the next page). If desired, use a few safety pins to roughly position the seed st strip so that it is evenly distributed around bag cover and ends in the equivalent spot, 1" (2.5cm) from last button hole on the other side.

With dpn, pick up 1 st from the seed st strip edge and 1 from the edge of the bag cover. K2 tog, k2 sts on dpn. Do not turn work. Bring yarn around the back of the work and start next row.

*Pick up 1 st each from the edge of both strip and the edge of the cover side, k2 tog, k2tog, k1. Bring yarn around.* Continue, rep between **.

When strip is attached to the bag cover, continue I-cord edging around the top edge of the cover, as follows:

*Pick up 1 st from edge of bag cover. Knit tog with one I-cord st. Knit the other 2 sts. Do not turn work. Bring yarn around back of work and start next row. Rep from *.

Continue across the top of the seed st strip and attach second side of bag cover to the strip in the same way as the first, continuing across the top edge of the cover side as well. To BO, k2tog, k1, BO.

At the end of this, one end of the seed st strip will not have attached I-cord. Attach yarn and work I-cord across last end of strip and BO as above.

Weave in ends.

## Finishing

Using a tapestry needle and matching yarn, work a whip st or blanket st around the edges of the buttonholes, taking care to adjust the holes to firmly fit around the bag's buttons.

Wet block again as necessary to avoid skewing.

When dry, attach cover to Bermuda Bag.

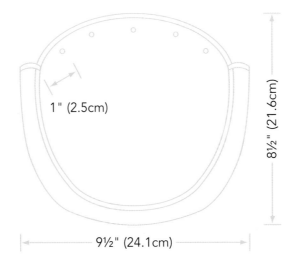

1" (2.5cm)

8½" (21.6cm)

9½" (24.1cm)

Pin Check Bermuda Bag

# Pin Check Bermuda Bag

Once you've mastered the Basic Bermuda Bag, it's time to branch out! Here's a slightly more complicated pattern that uses many of the same techniques as the basic bag and allows you to get lots of use out of your new purse. After a bit of knitting, you'll end up with a tweedy two-color organic cotton cover that matches multiple outfits. A bonus is that all your belongings stay inside the very same purse while you just switch the cover. It's a clever way to stay fashionable without extra work! (And of course, knitting is fun, and who can stop at just one or two covers?)

## Skill Level

Intermediate

## Size

One size fits the Jesse B. Collection Bermuda bag as specified below.

## Finished Measurements

Oblong measuring approximately 9½" (24.1cm) wide × 8½" (21.6cm) long

## Materials

- Color A: 2 skeins of Lion Brand Organic Cotton yarn, 100 percent Organic Cotton, 82 yd. (75m), 1¾ oz. (50g), color 003 Bark
- Color B: 1 skein of Lion Brand Organic Cotton yarn, 100 percent Organic Cotton, 82 yd. (75m), 1¾ oz. (50g), color 002 Almond

or

- Color A: 164 yd. (150m) of any worsted weight yarn with the appropriate gauge
- Color B: 82 yd. (75m) of any worsted weight yarn with the appropriate gauge
- U.S. size 6 (4mm) straight or circular needles, *or size to obtain gauge*
- U.S. size 6 (4mm) double-pointed needles, *or size to obtain gauge*
- Row counter
- Tapestry needle
- The Jesse B. Collection Bermuda Bag

**note** This pattern is designed to fit the Jesse B. Collection Bermuda Bag. This bag is manufactured in Pennsylvania and available in the United States. There are a wide variety of other similar bags available for sale and in thrift stores. While these bags will be a reasonable substitute, their measurements may vary. Acquire and examine your bag before casting on and adjust sizing and buttonhole placements accordingly.

## Gauge

19 sts and 40 rows = 4" (10cm) in pin check
20 sts and 36 rows = 4" (10cm) in seed stitch

## Pattern Stitches

### Pin Check

**Row 1 (WS):** With A, purl

**Row 2:** With Color B, k1, *sl1 wyib, k1, rep from *.

**Row 3:** With Color B, k1, *sl1 wyif, k1, rep from *.

**Row 4:** With Color A, knit.

### Seed Stitch

Worked over an even number of sts.

**Row 1 (RS):** *K1, p1; rep from * across.

**Row 2:** Knit the purl sts and purl the knit sts.
Rep row 2 for seed st.

## Instructions

**note** If you need to adjust the spacing of the buttonholes to fit a differently shaped Bermuda bag, remember to BO on Row 4 and CO on Row 1. This creates a tidy buttonhole in one color.

### Bag Cover Side (Make Two)

With Color A and straight or circular needles, CO 19 sts.

With Color A, work Row 1 of Pin Check patt.

Maintaining Pin Check patt so Color A creates straight lines of slip sts, inc 1 st at beg and end of each row. This will require you to alternate between k1 and sl1 st on Rows 2 and 3 as you inc. (I-cord worked later will hide these increases, so don't be concerned if the patt isn't maintained perfectly.)

Continue to inc, working 8 rows Pin Check patt for a total of 35 sts on the needle, ending after Row 1.

Work 6 more rows of Pin Check patt without inc, ending after Row 3.

## Make First Buttonhole

**Row 4:** With Color A, k2, BO 2, knit until end of row.

**Row 1 (WS):** P31, CO 2, p2.

**Row 2:** Maintaining Pin Check patt, inc 1 st at beg and end of each row for a total of 37 sts on the needle.

Work 9 more rows of Pin Check patt, beg with and ending after Row 3.

## Buttonhole #2

**Row 4:** *With Color A, k2, BO 2, knit until end of row.

**Row 1 (WS):** P33, CO 2, p2.

Work 10 rows Pin Check patt, ending after Row 3.*

## Buttonhole #3

Rep between ** above one more time to form Buttonhole #3.

## Buttonhole #4

**Row 4:** With Color A, k2, BO 2, knit until end of row.

**Row 1 (WS):** P33, CO 2, p2.

Work 9 more rows Pin Check patt, ending after Row 2.

### Decrease Row:

**Row 3 (WS):** Maintaining Pin Check patt, dec 1 st at each end of row (35 sts).

## Buttonhole #5

**Row 4:** With Color A, k2, BO 2, knit until end of row.

**Row 1 (WS):** P31, CO 2, p2.

**Row 2:** Work Pin Check patt Row 2.

Beg with Row 3, maintaining Pin Check patt, dec 1 st at beg and end of each row for 8 rows, until 19 sts rem.

Work Rows 3 and 4 of Pin Check patt with rem 19 sts.

BO with Color A.

Wet Block both sides of cover by washing or dampening at this point. Block these before adding I-cord edging as described below.

## Seed Stitch Strip

Follow instructions as specified in Basic Bermuda Bag pattern.

## Create Attached I-Cord Edging

Refer to instructions for attached I-cord edging section in Basic Bermuda Bag pattern.

## Finishing

Weave in ends.

Using tapestry needle and matching yarn, work a whip st or blanket st around the edges of the buttonholes, taking care to adjust the holes to firmly fit around the bag's buttons.

Wet block again. This helps adjust the fabric to its rounded, bag form and creates a crisp looking cotton cover.

When dry, attach cover to Bermuda Bag.

**note** Please consult the Basic Bermuda Bag pattern to see a schematic for this pattern; although the patterning is different, these bag covers are similar in size.

*A flax field being harvested in Normandy, France.*

Vegan
Knitting

At first glance, the topic of veganism doesn't seem to have much to do with knitting. Yet many vegans and some vegetarians try to go beyond just considering what they eat. In fact, some of them will be trying to pursue something that's called a "vegan (or vegetarian) lifestyle." First, it might be helpful to start with a definition or two.

A *vegetarian* is usually someone who chooses not to eat meat or fish of any kind. However, most vegetarians are *ovo-lacto vegetarians*, meaning they eat eggs and milk. Their decision to skip the hamburger in favor of a veggie burger may be health related—perhaps their family has a history of high cholesterol. It may also be religiously motivated. Many Hindus and Buddhists choose not to eat meat, and some traditions in Judaism and Christianity have periods of time each year when some may choose to avoid meat as part of a ritual observance. There are also vegetarians who choose not to eat meat or use leather, or any animal product that results from the slaughter of animals.

Vegans take this further and choose not to eat or use anything that comes from an animal. The Vegan Society, founded in 1944, explains it this way, "A *vegan* is someone who tries to live without exploiting animals, for the benefit of animals, people, and the planet. Vegans eat a plant-based diet, with nothing coming from animals—no meat, milk, eggs, or honey, for example. A vegan lifestyle also avoids leather, wool, silk, and other animal products for clothing or any other purpose." Historically, many religious groups have had similar diets, including some Buddhists, Eastern Orthodox Christians, Jains, Hindus, Sikhs, Rastafarians, and Seventh-Day Adventists. The Vegan Society explains the reasons behind this choice today by saying "People avoid animal products for ethical, health, and environmental reasons. You can free up crops to feed hungry people, and reduce your contribution to animal suffering and global climate change by choosing a plant-based diet."

Now, what does it have to do with you? Well, you might be a vegan knitter! If not, consider that most knitters have the chance to knit for others. What should we choose to knit for vegans? Are there yarn choices that are more or less appropriate? Which of these choices are sustainable yarns?

## What Are Appropriate Vegan Yarn Choices?

Vegans may choose not to wear anything that comes from an animal. This will mean, for instance, that wool, silk, alpaca, llama, cashmere, Pygora, qiviut, and Angora are out of the question! No suede leather slipper bottoms or horn buttons would be appropriate.

If you're taking a long time to knit for someone who has this philosophy, there's no point in spending a lot of time on a garment the person will never wear. What are other options?

## Natural Fibers

Many people divide fiber choices into three categories: natural fibers, synthetic fibers, and man-made fibers. In terms of natural fibers, some good choices for vegan knitting include organic hemp, cotton, flax (also called linen), and ramie. Of course, conventionally farmed cotton uses a lot of pesticide and fertilizer, which, as mentioned earlier, isn't good for the environment. Also, many of these fibers may be transported over long distances (think of all that gas!) to arrive at your knitting store. As long as you choose yarns from these natural fibers that are raised sustainably and preferably organically, you're making a fine choice.

## Synthetic Fibers

Synthetic fibers are also popular, accounting for a little more than half of global fiber production. Synthetics, also known by the names of polyester, nylon, and acrylic, are created from petroleum. These yarns often wear like iron, can be reused or recycled, and are machine washable. Synthetics are inexpensive. According to some sources, synthetics are made from byproducts of the petroleum industry. Thus, as long as oil is being consumed at a high rate, this type of fiber might be a way to use that byproduct and to avoid letting a precious resource go to waste.

As recent rising fuel costs can attest however, the use of petroleum is not sustainable. That is,

we have a limited amount of it available to us on Earth. It takes even more petroleum energy for the process that converts petrochemicals into fiber. Although the process takes little water, unlike irrigated cotton, for instance, the heavy chemicals used in this process have great potential for environmental pollution to the air and water if these were to leak or be dumped before treatment. Finally, that hardwearing yarn doesn't breathe well while one is wearing it, and the yarn lasts forever, literally. Synthetics don't biodegrade well, which means that long after we've stopped enjoying that bright orange 70s era granny square afghan, it will still be around, if not at our house, then perhaps at the local landfill. Choosing a new synthetic yarn has some advantages, and some serious disadvantages.

## Man-Made Fibers

The third category of yarn, man-made fibers, is a complex one. There are a lot of fibers on the market these days that are billed as "eco-friendly" or "made of renewable resources" such as soy silk, bamboo, corn, or wood. These are all cellulose fibers and start with an agricultural product. Both soy and corn are pesticide- and fertilizer-intensive crops, so it helps to find out if the source crops for these yarns are raised organically or sustainably. When it comes to bamboo or wood, we have to look for companies that only harvest these crops with care...wholesale destruction of a forest, for instance, is not a good outcome for any knitter to consider!

While yarn producers view their production of these textiles as proprietary information, there are some details that we know. For instance, in the yarn advertisements, bamboo is always billed as "eco-friendly" and "renewable." These yarns are biodegradable, and offer, in some formulations, beautiful shine and drape to the finished fabric.

There are three types of man-made cellulosic fiber categories: viscose (or rayon), modal, and lyocell. These are different generations of fibers—rayon, for instance, was developed over a hundred years ago. Modal (usually sourced from beech trees) was developed next. Lyocell (also called Tencel) is a newer kind of man-made fiber, also somewhat better for the environment than viscose/rayon or modal. All of these yarns begin by breaking down the cell walls of a plant fiber, like trees, bamboo, soy, corn, etc. Some of these raw materials come from waste products, such as the byproducts of the making of tofu, in the case of soy.

Amanda Berka's article, "Where it Comes From: Regenerated Fibers," in *Interweave Knits* magazine's Summer 2008 issue explains the process. In summary, heat or chemicals break down the raw "mulch" and this produces a liquid. This is put through a nozzle with little holes to form strands. This "cures" into a solid thread, which is then spun and further processed into plied yarn.

The production processes of man-made fibers have different environmental impacts. Modal and rayon/viscose use a lot of water in their production and the newer Lyocell uses less. Both modal and rayon/viscose are fairly chemical and energy intensive, and emissions from this process to water can result in high pollution. Lyocell, the newest process, is more environmentally friendly, with complete biodegradability and a nontoxic and noncorrosive process, according to Kate Fletcher's analysis in *Sustainable Fashion & Textiles: Design Journeys* (Earthscan, 2008).

The biggest concerns with all of these yarns are the energy it takes to produce them. Whether it's coal or petroleum that powers the production facilities, it's a manufacturing process that's energy intensive and can sometimes pollute water with chemicals. Many industrialized countries have careful legal protocols to protect from chemical pollution to the environment, but not all third world countries (where these fibers may be produced) have such strong environmental standards in place.

The most interesting details I found about the production of bamboo yarns are the ones we don't see. For instance, some companies advertise bamboo itself as antibacterial, but these properties vary when processed into yarn. Although the general conclusion is that there are some antimicrobial properties to bamboo, studies seem to differ as to its effectiveness in warding off bacteria. Also, bamboo yarn, manufactured in China, can be broken down and processed chemically or with mechanized equipment. The end product looks exactly the same. The chemical process offers a risk of environmental pollution, as mentioned previously.

The mechanized equipment can break down the bamboo into a powder without any risk of chemical pollution. However, the mechanized approach is several times more expensive than the chemical process, and consumers predictably choose the less expensive product. The hope in the future is that there will be a way to show the consumer which kinds of bamboo are produced in the most sustainable fashion, so we'll know which kinds of bamboo yarns "tread lightly on the earth."

Vegan knitters are often at the forefront when it comes to exploring new yarns and fibers not produced by an animal. Thanks to their efforts, knitters are much more aware of many of the possibilities available for all of us! Even so, it's best to question critically when it comes to new products. The advertising that encourages knitters to believe that something is sustainable or good for the earth may overstate the environmental benefits of the newer man-made fibers. It doesn't mean we shouldn't try all these exciting yarns, but occasionally, the energy cost of some of the newer man-made vegan fibers may outstrip any benefits in terms of carbon footprint. These choices are hard to quantify—and we must consider, as individuals, if they are worth the cost.

Zigzag Butterfly
Table Runner

# Zigzag Butterfly Table Runner

Choosing a project that uses vegan fibers can sometimes be easy because the fiber is the most logical choice! Marriage is full of twists and turns and this runner, knit in a zigzag pattern is the perfect gift for a new couple. While I originally designed this as a table runner for a wedding present, it also makes a very elegant lace scarf. This project uses linen because it is machine washable and dryable and will be durable and elegant for anyone's table (or neck!) over the years. Its interesting shape with the gently sloping butterfly edges is formed through the creative use of needle sizes in conjunction with the pattern. The pattern starts with a U.S. size 8 (5mm) needle, and after one repeat, it changes to a U.S. size 6 (4mm). After another repeat, it changes to a U.S. size 4 (3.5mm.) Like marriage, the challenges change over time, but the sum of the shapes remains the same. In our family, some of the most important things take place over meals (even vegan ones), so why not have a metaphor for those meaningful zigs and zags on your dining room table? The table runner measures 40" × 5½" (101.6cm × 14cm) wide, with the blocked gauge transitioning from 2.85 sts to the inch (2.54cm) on a size 8 needle to 3.5 sts to an inch (2.54cm) on a size 4 needle.

## Skill Level

Intermediate

## Size

One size

## Finished Measurements

40" × 5½" (101.6cm × 14cm) after blocking

## Materials

**note** One skein of Euroflax makes two table runners.

- 1 skein of Euroflax Sport Weight yarn, 100 percent Linen (flax), 270 yd. (247m), 3½ oz. (100g), color 52 Grape

or

- 135 yd. (124m) of any sportweight yarn with the appropriate gauge
- U.S. size 8 (5 mm) needles, straight or 24" (61cm) circular needle

- U.S. size 6 (4 mm) needles, straight or 24" (61cm) circular needle
- U.S. size 4 (3.5 mm) needles, straight or 24" (61cm) circular needle
- Row counter
- Tapestry needle
- Blocking wires or straight pins for blocking

## Gauge

**note** Blocked gauge transitions with the change in needle sizes, and this size change in the finished piece causes the fabric to draw in and the gauges to shift slightly. Over 4" (10cm), measured on a blocked swatch knitted solely on the specified needles:

11.5 sts = 4" (10cm) on #8 (5mm) needles in Zigzag Butterfly patt

14 sts = 4" (10cm) on #4 (3.5mm) needles

To check gauge, knit a small swatch in Zigzag Butterfly patt and block.

## Pattern Stitches

### Zigzag Butterfly

Worked over an even number of sts.

**Row 1 (WS) and all WS rows:** Purl.

**Row 2, 4, and 6 (RS):** K1, *yo, k2tog; rep from *, end sl1 st pwise.

**Row 8, 10, and 12 (RS):** K1, *ssk, yo; rep from *, end k1.

## Instructions

With #8 (5mm) needles, CO 120 sts.

Using row counter, work 12 rows or 1 rep of Zigzag Butterfly patt.

Switch to #6 (4mm) needles, work 2nd rep of Zigzag Butterfly patt (Rows 13–24).

Switch to #4 (3.75mm) needles, work 3rd rep of Zigzag Butterfly patt (Rows 25–36).

BO pwise.

## Finishing

Weave in ends.

To block linen or other plant fibers:

Immerse in water, wring out gently, and block on a towel or blocking board to appropriate size. Use blocking wires or pins to create the butterfly zigzag edge. Allow to dry.

40" (101.6cm)

5½" (14cm)

Vegan Security Blankie

# Vegan Security Blankie

If you're a beginning knitter or one who doesn't mind a long stretch of garter stitch, this project's for you! This blankie is the right size for a baby's stroller or car seat. Knit in strips and joined by bright whip stitching, this vegan yarn is entirely machine washable. It's also designed so that as the child ages, the blanket can be reduced in size (just rip out the whip stitch) so that a toddler or preschooler can carry around a part while the other part is in the wash! This is the ultimate security—you'll always have a piece of the blankie on hand for comforting worried little ones.

## Skill Level
Beginner

## Size
One size

## Finished Measurements
Approximately 20" × 27½" (50.8cm × 69.9cm)

Each strip of knitting will measure approximately 5½" × 20" (14cm × 51cm)

## Materials
Used double:
- Color A: 5 skeins of Crystal Palace Panda Cotton yarn, 55 percent Bamboo, 24 percent Cotton, 21 percent Elastic Nylon, 182 yd. (166.4m), 1¾ oz. (50g), color 2302 Baby Blues

**note** The color palette of this yarn has shifted slightly since this design was created. A good blue substitute would be color 0202 Dotty Blues, with 7189 New Blues as a darker alternative.

- Color B: 3 skeins of Crystal Palace Maizy yarn, 82 percent Corn Fiber, 18 percent Elastic Nylon, 204 yd. (186.5m), 1¾ oz. (50g), color 0204 Ivory White
- Colors C and D: 1 skein each of Crystal Palace Bamboozle yarn, 55 percent Bamboo, 24 percent Cotton, 21 percent Elastic Nylon, 90 yd. (82.3m) 1¾ oz. (50g), color 7063 Dutch Blue *and* 0211 Lacquer Red

or

- Color A: 910 yd. (832m) machine washable fingering weight yarn with the appropriate gauge (worked double)
- Color B: 612 yd. (566m) machine washable fingering weight yarn with the appropriate gauge (worked double)

or

- Color A: 455 yd. (416m) machine washable light worsted weight or DK yarn with the appropriate gauge
- Color B: 306 yd. (283m) machine washable light worsted weight or DK yarn with the appropriate gauge

and

- Colors C and D: part of 1 skein each machine washable worsted weight yarn, smooth enough for sewing whip st and connecting the knitted strips.
- U.S. size 6 (4mm) circular or straight needles, *or size to obtain gauge*
- Tapestry needle

## Gauge

22 sts and 40 rows = 4" (10cm) in garter stitch

## Instructions

### Knit Three Strips with Color A (Blue)

With fingering weight yarn doubled or one strand of light worsted or DK weight yarn, CO 30 sts.

Knit every row until last st. With yarn in front, slip last st pwise for a neat edge.

Work until strip measures 20" (51cm).

BO.

### Knit Two Strips with Color B (White)

Work as for Color A strips above.

### Finishing

Weave in ends.

Line up strips, and alternate by color, as in diagram. Using Color C and a tapestry needle, work whip st in one direction to join strips. Use as many sts as necessary to firmly attach strips together; the diagram sts are just to illustrate the X technique. Using Color D, work whip st in the opposite direction, creating X shapes as a decorative finish on the blanket. Continue in this fashion to join the strips together.

To block, wash the blanket according to yarn label instructions and lay flat to dry. This way it will be clean and ready for the new arrival!

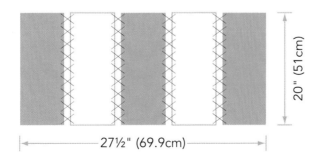

20" (51cm)

27½" (69.9cm)

# Maintaining Folk and Indigenous Traditions

Have you ever encountered a yarn with a label that says, "With the purchase of this yarn, you're supporting...." Did that notion sway you toward buying the yarn? Many knitters are attracted to purchasing yarns or choosing knitting products that "make a difference." That positive difference might mean supporting people's traditions and livelihoods in your neighborhood or across the planet. Perhaps you'd like to know the money you spend on your hobby also goes to support something you value.

As the world becomes increasingly globalized, many folk traditions that involve textiles may disappear. While we know that small-scale, environmentally friendly co-ops and family businesses are likely the best way to purchase our fiber, sometimes it's hard to find or prioritize this. When it's easier to buy something mass produced, these highly individualized traditions can be lost. We've all faced this. When it is less expensive to buy something you need than it is to make it, we begin to lose the skills to spin and/or knit our own garments.

Sometimes, enterprising individuals and communities work against this trend, and they create a global market for a particularly special indigenous fiber arts tradition. We often jump immediately to the well–known, third world co-operatives that create yarns and knitted or woven items now available at your yarn store. However, we can start right in our own communities.

A few years ago, my husband and I visited my parents' West Virginia vacation home. On the drive back to Kentucky, we stopped at an artists' community called Penn Alps, in Grantsville, Maryland. While we were there,

we met John Childers, the miller who ran Stanton's Mill, the stone ground grist mill on site. It took no time at all to discover that John Childers grew up in Eastern Kentucky. In only a few minutes, we found we had something else in common. John is a spinner. He isn't just any kind of spinner. He's possibly one of the last indigenous old time Kentucky spinners.

Eastern Kentucky, well known for its Appalachian poverty, took a long time to become modernized. Inaccessible rural communities continued to do things the way they always had—including spinning and weaving for their own households. Many communities lacked electricity, indoor plumbing and other niceties until well past the end of World War II. As soon as it became possible to access industrially made yarns and fabrics, the spinning wheels and looms were moved directly to the barn…this was one chore that overworked women could discard.

John Childers' family continued to spin and weave. Their particular specialty was a type of traditional woven coverlet, usually done in white and blue, or white and red. These coverlets, woven by this family, are now on display in museums, including the Smithsonian.

*A young shepherdess helps to bring in sheep on Britain's Fair Isle.*

We were welcomed into this man's home to see his great wheel, and to admire his finely spun single ply yarns.

We lived in Kentucky for several years and people from other areas of the country often asked me about the Appalachian spinning and weaving traditions. I usually explained what locals explained to me—that in an age of big box stores, few people bothered to value local handiwork or handicrafts. Those skills gradually disappear, because the number of practitioners age or decline and the knowledge is eventually lost.

After many years and only by happenstance, I came across the last vestige of the rich textile tradition of Kentucky Appalachia, which is embodied in perhaps a single person who has moved out of the state. Perhaps the last indigenous old time spinner in Kentucky lives in Maryland, and dreams of moving home to Kentucky. John Childers, former Weaver Laureate of Kentucky, continues the tradition for his own enjoyment and the occasional museum coverlet.

This quick loss of historic traditions to globalism isn't limited to areas with big box stores. In Hania, a city on the island of Crete, in Greece, the local rug weaving tradition (and its attendant skills) is dying off. On a visit to Crete, we encountered only one active weaving workshop, in which family members raise sheep, spin, and dye wool for the family's looms. While there are lots of stunning rugs in antique stores, if you want an authentic new one, there are very few places to purchase a rug. Sadly, even this one rug weaving workshop couldn't earn enough money to support its master weaver, who worked an outside job to financially maintain his family's shop.

When yarns, knitted, and woven goods are produced in your own community, there are a variety of advantages. First, it reduces the enormous cost of transportation costs. Globalization means that your socks may be made less expensively, but just imagine the fuel used to transport them from the other side of the world! Another advantage is an economic one. When you spend money in your community, those local workers can then buy other local products, thus keeping your local economy healthy. If you buy those socks made in a third-world country, not much of that money will stay in your town's economy, and far less of it will make it back to the town in China where the socks were produced.

Another advantage, the one I've sketched out earlier, is that of maintaining the diversity of our textile traditions. Rugs woven in Crete or an Appalachian coverlet are unique items, special to their regions. If you're proud of where you come from, you might be proud enough of your region's rich textile history and creativity to help financially support its future.

If supporting and maintaining the rich folk traditions and indigenous skills of spinning, knitting, and weaving are important to you, how can you help?

## Help Local Artisans Turn a Profit

In many cases, helping individual artisans earn a living helps maintain their traditional skills in a community setting. In New Mexico, the scenic high road to Taos goes through Chimayo, an important historic center for Classic Rio Grande (Hispanic) weaving. This form of fiber

▲ *For centuries, herding dogs have been a traditional part of shepherding.*

arts, defined by the early Spanish settlers 500 years ago, starts with the rare breed of Navajo-Churro sheep and proceeds through hand spinning, natural dyes, and a highly skilled kind of weaving. These weavers usually work with a stand-up walking loom, also known as a Rio Grande, as compared to the Anglo floor loom, where one weaves while seated.

In the twenty-first century media age, it can be hard to comprehend the value of this kind of work. However, a clever combination of both publicity and rarity make these rugs famous and highly sought after by collectors. That popularity and cachet keep individual weavers

and their families afloat and allow them to maintain a valuable regional artistic tradition.

Many weavers in this area of New Mexico win national awards for their work, and the region is known for the rich resources of multiple generations of skilled weavers. I learned about this by visiting a variety of studios as well as Santa Fe's Spanish Market, which shows off the works of many talented weavers. Later, I took the high road to Taos myself and stopped by some of these traditional weaving studios, where one can see photos and rugs that link multigenerational families. In particular, I had the luck to see a whole wall of photographs, an old spinning wheel, and a hand-built loom at Centinela Traditional Arts in Chimayo, where Irvin Trujillo, recent National Heritage Fellowship Award winner and seventh generation weaver, works with his wife, accomplished spinner and weaver, Lisa Trujillo. Mr. Trujillo's work is on display in the Museum of American History in Washington, D.C.

As individuals, we can choose something precious, like a handwoven rug, to decorate our homes. As knitters, we can support a rare breed of sheep like the Navajo Churro by knitting something hardwearing from yarn spun from its valuable fleece. By economically supporting artisans whose history we value, we can help maintain their know-how in the next generation.

## Support a Co-Op

You may know about co-ops as a source for inexpensive groceries. The first co-operative organizations were started by fiber artists, such the Fenwick Weavers' Society in Scotland in 1761. This organization of weavers got together to purchase bulk food items and books. The notion of a co-operative today goes far beyond food. Any group that joins together to meet economic and social needs through a jointly owned and democratically run enterprise can be called a co-operative. Today many of these organizations help communities maintain a rich fiber arts tradition.

Continuing with the Southwest traditions, one can support organizations such as Tierra Wools. Tierra Wools is owned by the wool growers, spinners, and weavers who help run the organization. Started as a way of keeping the Rio Grande weaving traditions alive, it serves as an important local business in Los Ojos, New

Mexico, bringing income, jobs, skills, and training to a rural area. Whether you buy yarn, a handwoven rug, or visit to take a spinning or weaving class, choosing to support a co-op can help maintain important local traditions.

If you happen to be in Vermont, you can visit an entirely different worker/owner co-operative. The Green Mountain Spinnery produces sumptuous knitting yarns and creative designs at its mill. Maintaining the textile mill tradition in New England, this small co-operative uses well cared for machinery that is up to a hundred years old. All the fiber it uses comes from the United States; its 100 percent wool yarns are all from New England wool. While its yarns are modern, rich in color, and produced in an environmentally sustainable manner, the mere existence of Green Mountain Spinnery's mill helps maintain a historic New England tradition.

## Buy from a Nonprofit

Nonprofit organizations also help to boost historic fiber arts traditions. Returning to New Mexico, you can't help but drop by the Española Valley Fiber Arts Center if you'd like a good learning experience or some bit of local fiber. This nonprofit center sells spinning wheels, looms, yarns, and Navajo-Churro wool to the community. It also teaches classes, and the warped looms that fill the back room are an inspiring mix of color and texture. Started in 1995 as a way to help locals learn how to use those looms they'd inherited, this fiber arts center helps promote a rich and historic textile history and help it grow.

Many other organizations that are nonprofit are also fair-trade. More information about this issue is included in the next chapter.

# Spend More to Maintain Historic Traditions

Sometimes the way to support a traditional way of life is to decide to purchase yarns and patterns even if they might seem more expensive. Many "foodies" choose to do this when they buy groceries that support smaller farms, even if the produce is perhaps more expensive than at the grocery store. There is a great value in supporting family farms. In the same way, we can choose knitting yarns that maintain a historic tradition.

A well-known example might be that of Shetland wool. This wool comes from Shetland sheep, a breed from the Shetland Islands. Until recently, the Rare Breeds Survival Trust in the United Kingdom classed this sheep breed as "rare," meaning the breed was considered endangered. Recently, there has been some improvement in the status of this breed because of increased support and interest in it. The perpetuation of the sheep breed is a wonderful step to maintain biodiversity, but the traditions of the Shetlanders are also something important to preserve. Shetland lace is a complicated and fascinating part of knitwear history and tradition. If you pursue it, you can choose to buy Shetland wools from the Shetland Islands to support the people who developed them! Better yet, if you feel Shetland lace is beyond your skills but want to purchase some, women in Shetland are still knitting this lace for sale as a way to support themselves in a far-flung part of Britain.

Ever heard of Fair Isle? This stranded knitting tradition comes from Fair Isle, one of the Shetland Islands. Again, choosing to knit with the yarns and patterns of the islands themselves supports the continuation of this tradition. We may call any stranded knitting tradition "Fair Isle" today, but it came from the Shetlands first! Shetland Island women still sell their hand-knitting and designs to make a living in the way they have for hundreds of years.

Another ancient and rare breed of island sheep made popular again is the Gotland sheep. Originally from the Island of Gotland, in Sweden, the Swedes decided to "improve" and change the breed beginning in the 1920s. There is a movement afoot to maintain the historic character of this sheep, and flocks have been established in Britain, the United States, Denmark, Australia, the Netherlands, and New Zealand to preserve its Scandinavian history and traditions.

Oddly, the thing that brought great success to Gotland breeders was the film production for the Lord of the Rings trilogy. The costumes were sourced from the famous 'Stansborough Grey' wool Gotland flock of Barry and Cheryl Eldridge in New Zealand. This wool is now available as fabric, yarn, and fleece and has achieved world famous status. Sometimes the way to rebuild a Scandinavian wool tradition is to build up a sheep breed (in other countries), create a fabulous product, and then sell it to Hollywood!

# Preserving Historic Knitting Traditions on a Budget

Some great natural fibers are available all over the world for a reasonable price. A special example is Lopi yarn from Iceland. A loosely spun single ply that comes in a fabulous array of colors, Lopi yarn is sourced exclusively from Icelandic sheep, another rare breed. The Icelandic wool is hardwearing, warm, and beautiful. Plus, Icelandic sheep are a triple purpose breed, producing good meat and milk for sheep's cheeses. In Iceland, traditional sweaters are still being designed and worn; and the sheep (which greatly out-number the people) bring food, work, and outside economic support to this small island country.

Another old standby is Briggs and Little yarn, produced by Briggs and Little Woolen Mill, the oldest woolen mill in Canada. The mill's produced yarn for sale since 1857. Located in New Brunswick, this mill uses only Canadian wool and is a Canadian knitwear tradition. Using environmentally friendly processing techniques, this mill is not just good for sup-porting the economy of its province but is well known for keeping generations of hand-knitting Canadians warm in their knitwear.

# ᔕ Stuffing ᔕ

Several projects in this book and chapter call for stuffing. Polyester based stuffing is always available at hobby and fabric stores for knitting projects. However, polyester is a petroleum based product, so you'll find I don't recommend using it in this book. Not only is the use of petroleum-based products not sustainable, but it's not always safe—it can be highly flammable, which can be very dangerous around children and pets. Now we realize there are better options (sometimes the traditional ones) for sustainability and safety.

## Wool

If you'd like a spongy, elastic filling that is naturally antibacterial and flame retardant, consider using wool. Clean wool roving or batting is available online, at local farms, and at handspinning shops. Ask for a medium to coarse wool, which will not felt with lots of use. In addition, these wools are usually less expensive than fine wools. If organic fibers are a priority, this isn't difficult, as organic wool is also easily obtainable online.

## Cotton

Cotton batting and stuffing is widely available. It's machine washable and popular for toys and pillows. Cotton does become compacted and hard over time, so it may not be ideal for projects that should be soft or springy in the long term. Although organic cotton batting or stuffing isn't in every store, it's available online and the best option in terms of sustainability if you're interested in using it. As mentioned earlier, conventionally grown cotton uses a lot of pesticides and fertilizers which not

Other cold climates have produced similarly hearty textiles. Harris Tweed is famous for its hand-woven wool and may well have been a staple of our grandfathers' closets. Yet, even today, the wool from the Hebrides Islands in Scotland is a great knitting staple—tweedy, rustic, affordable, and fabulous for men's knitting garments.

Let's not limit ourselves to wool! Think llama and alpaca yarn is only for the wealthy? In South America, these fibers are bringing economic stimulation to the people who raise the animals and spin the yarns. Due to the lower cost of living in South America, these camelid fibers look remarkably affordable when sold in the United States. Also, this new interest in llamas and alpacas has helped maintain a rich and ancient South American textile tradition. Read more about this topic in chapter 5, as many of these programs are also Fair Trade ones.

only pollute water ways and ecosystems, but also can be harmful to people. If you want your child or pet to cuddle up to something with cotton stuffing, organic is the best—and reasonably affordable—way to go.

## Bamboo

Bamboo stuffing and bamboo blends are now available for sale at many stores. This stuffing may be antibacterial and is easy to find. Bamboo itself is a sustainably harvested material, and its fibers are easily washed, warm, and antistatic. However, the process of creating bamboo fiber from the plants themselves is an energy-intensive one that is not necessarily environmentally friendly. (See chapter 3 for more details.)

## Rag Stuffing

Got any worn out T-shirts around? How about a moth-eaten wool sweater from the local thrift store? Rag stuffing is a great chance to reuse material, save money, and work toward sustainability. Cotton rags make a good, dense material, ideal for hard felted projects or things that don't need elasticity. You can combine different rags, putting cotton in as a "core" and then using more spongy materials (such as an old wool sweater) around it to have both a firm core and a springy stuffing. When stuffing with rags, take care to know the fiber content of your stuffing (polyester is still flammable, even when reusing it!) and the end use of your project. Dog toys, for instance, run the risk of being chewed open...and in this case, it is best to use large pieces of rag so you can take away the stuffing before your pet may ingest it. Softer stuffing can be produced by cutting up rags into little pieces. Experiment to create the kind of affordable stuffing your project needs and you'd prefer.

**Math Mobile**

# Math Mobile

This fast-to-knit mobile is interesting to make and ideal for an infant. For your next baby shower, consider natural-colored Shetland yarns knit into small geometric objects that hang from a handmade mobile. The basic colors will appeal to an infant's developing vision, and the organic, nondyed materials and shape identification will appeal to the baby's mom. Purchasing the yarns used in the sample allows a knitter to support Shetland Islands' natives and the perpetuation of the Shetland sheep breed, as well.

## Skill Level
Easy

## Size
One size

## Finished Measurements
Approximately 18" (45.7cm) in length × 13" (33cm) wide (overall, assembled)

Individual knitted objects are approximately 2" × 2" (5cm × 5cm) to 2" × 3½" (5cm × 8.9cm)

## Materials
- 1 skein each of Yarns International Shetland 2000 yarn, 100 percent Shetland wool, 190 yd. (173.7m), 1¾ oz. (50g), color Shetland Black 2005 (Color A) and Shetland White 2001 (Color B)

or

- 190 yd. (173.7m) each of any fingering weight yarn in 2 contrasting colors with the appropriate gauge
- U.S. size 3 (3.25mm) straight or circular needles, 16" (40.6cm) long, *or size to obtain gauge*
- U.S. size 3 (3.25mm) double-pointed needles, *or size to obtain gauge*
- Stitch markers
- Row counter
- Wool Roving or Batts or Organic Cotton Stuffing (see previous page for more information on environmentally friendly stuffing)
- Tapestry needle
- ⅜" (9mm) or ¼" (6mm) dowel or stick, 12½" (31.8cm) long
- 2 wooden beads with inside hole that fits around dowel or stick with a little room to spare (enough to fit a layer of ribbon)
- 1 yd. (1m) ⅜" (9mm) double-sided ribbon
- Wood glue

## Gauge

24 sts and 32 rows = 4" (10cm) in stockinette stitch

# Instructions

**note** Mobiles are infinitely flexible in size and shape. If your dowel size, stitch gauge, or ribbon length varies from the following, the project will still come out well! Take care to be sure everything is firmly attached to the mobile and that it is well out of reach for any baby's curious hands. Otherwise, let your creativity take flight and enjoy making a toy!

## Ball Bauble

With Color A and dpns, CO 2 sts on each of 4 needles for a total of 8 sts.

Join, pm, and working in the round, knit 1 rnd.

**Make 1 Rnd:** On each needle, make 1 by kf&b in first st and last st on each needle. For this first rnd, you will work kf&b on every st, for a total of 4 sts on each needle. At the end of rnd, there will be 16 sts.

**Rnd 1:** Knit even.

**Rnd 2:** Knit make 1 rnd as above, making 1 st at beg and end of each needle.

Work Rnds 1 and 2 one more time, for a total of 32 sts.

Knit 5 rnds even.

## Work Decreases

**Rnd 1:** *K2tog, knit until last 2 sts on the needle, ssk.* Rep between * and * for each needle until end of rnd.

**Rnd 2:** Knit even.

Work Rnds 1 and 2 one more time; 16 sts rem.

Insert stuffing into Ball Bauble until it is rounded and soft.

Work Rnds 1 and 2 once more; 8 sts rem.

**Next Rnd:** k2tog on each needle for a total of 4 sts.

**Final Rnd:** Slipping sts to same needle as required, k2tog twice for a total of 2 sts on 1 dpn.

CO additional 2 sts, for a total of 4 sts on 1 dpn.

## Work I-Cord

With rem 4 sts, work I-cord for 5" (12.7cm).

## Divide I-Cord into Two

Divide I-cord sts by putting 2 sts on each of 2 dpns. Beg with the dpn with the yarn attached to it, work a 2 st I-cord of 1½" (3.8cm) or length to tie around dowel. BO.

Join yarn to second 2-st section of I-cord, work as first. BO.

Your I-cord should look like the letter Y.

## Finishing

Weave in ends.

## Triangle Bauble

With straight or circular needles, and Color B, CO 16 sts.

Knit 2 rows.

Working in St st, continue until work measures 2¾" (7cm) (piece is approximately square). End after purl row.

Purl 1 Row.

BO pwise all but 4 sts. Knit to end of row.

Transfer rem 4 sts to a dpn. As described
for Ball Bauble, work I-cord for 4" (10cm)
then divide and work Y with each end
1½" (3.8cm) or length to tie around
dowel. BO.

## Sew Triangle

Fold square in half diagonally, matching
point of square with I-cord to opposite
point, to make triangle shape. With a
tapestry needle and matching yarn, sew
up one side with whip st. Stuff triangle
until rounded and soft. Sew second side.

## Finishing

Weave in ends.

## Square Bauble #1

With straight or circular needles and Color B,
CO 12 sts.

Knit 2 rows.

Work St st for 14 rows.

With Color A, Work 15 rows St st.

K2 rows.

BO 8 sts.

Transfer rem 4 sts to a dpn. As described
for Ball Bauble, work I-cord with Color A
for 2½" (6.4cm), then divide and work Y
with each end 1½" (3.8cm) or length to
tie around dowel. BO.

## Sew Square

Using a tapestry needle and matching
yarn, use whip st to sew square together
on two sides. Stuff until rounded and
soft. Sew up last side.

## Finishing

Weave in ends.

## Square Bauble #2

Work as for Square Bauble #1, reversing
Colors A and B.

## Finishing

Weave in ends.

Fold ribbon in half and make a slip knot
"loop" in the middle of the ribbon.
Thread ribbon ends through beads and
tie a knot at each end. Thread beads
onto ends of dowel, with ribbon inside.
Adjust it to hang neatly. Use glue to
firmly attach beads and ribbon ends to
dowel.

When glue is dry, tie the baubles firmly
with a double knot on the dowel in any
pleasing arrangement. Hang slip knot
loop from a hook in the ceiling so that,
for safety's sake, the baby cannot reach
the mobile under any circumstances.

Knick Knack Paddy
Whack Dog Toys

# Knick Knack Paddy Whack Dog Toys

Give a dog a bone? Dogs carry their toys around in their mouths. Wouldn't it be better if those toys were made of natural, organic, and safe fibers? Many dyes can also be harmful to dogs or humans if ingested, and it's hard not to ingest things when they're in your mouth! This led me to design with organic, natural-colored fibers. Here you'll find two options for each toy—a felted and a nonfelted option, which are easy to adjust in size if your dog prefers something smaller or larger. If your Fido is a big chewer, go straight to the felted option, and felt your toy hard to prevent damage. If your dog is a more dainty Fifi and doesn't destroy her toys, the nonfelted option is for you. You might add a bell or squeaker inside the stuffing if you're sure that it won't be unsafe for your dog's chewing habits.

As with any dog toy, watch for any damage and mend or remove the toy from your dog so it won't ingest pieces of stuffing or knitting. Bone is designed for those who enjoy carrying one around and chewing, and Fetch is for those with retrievers. (You know who you are.) The felted version is firmer, but the nonfelted version, stuffed with wool, is great for those who drool to excess. Wool can hold a lot of moisture and can handle a hand washing or two. Enjoy playing with environmentally friendly and dog-safe toys—and remember, no dog toy lasts forever. Inspect your toy frequently to be sure your Fido or Fifi will be safe.

## Skill Level

Easy

## Size

S—unfelted (L—felted)

## Finished Measurements

Bone: After stuffing, approximately 7½ (9½)" (19 [24]cm) long × 3 (4)" (7.6 [10.2]cm) wide at the edges.

Fetch: After stuffing, approximately 11 (10½)" (28 [26.5]cm) long × 3½ (4½)" (8.9 [11.4]cm) wide

Approximate length and width of Bone and Fetch projects before felting:

Bone: 10" (25.4cm) long × 4½" (11.4cm) wide at edge

Fetch: 12" (30.5cm) long × 4⅓" (10.9cm) wide

## Materials

- Color A: 1 skein of Green Mountain Spinnery Maine Organic Worsted yarn, 100 percent wool, 250 yd. (228.6m), 4 oz. (113.4g), color White (for Bone)
- Color B: 1 skein of Green Mountain Spinnery Maine Organic Worsted yarn, 100 percent wool, 250 yd. (228.6m), 4 oz. (113.4g), color Dark (for Fetch)
- Color C: 1 skein of Green Mountain Spinnery Maine Organic Worsted yarn, 100 percent wool, 250 yd. (228.6m), 4 oz. (113.4g), color Grey (for Fetch)

or

- 3 skeins of 250 yd. (228.6m) each of any natural-colored worsted weight yarns with the appropriate gauge (1 skein of a single color for Bone; 2 skeins of contrasting colors for Fetch)
- U.S. size 2 (2.5mm or 2.75mm) double-pointed needles, *or size to obtain gauge*
- U.S. size 7 (4.5mm) double-pointed needles, *or size to obtain gauge*
- Stitch markers
- Row counter
- Tapestry needle
- Squeaker or bell (optional)
- Stuffing: Old cotton T-shirts or rags or medium to coarse wool roving or batting (see note)

**note** To create a firm felted Bone or Fetch, large pieces of old T-shirts or other cotton jersey fabric make great stuffing and are a good way to reuse something and reduce waste. Take care not to use very small pieces of rag as these could endanger your dog if he or she pulls the toy apart. To create an ultra-absorbent and squishy nonfelted toy, use medium to coarse wool roving or batting. Avoid fine wools such as Merino because they will felt with frequent playtime.

## Gauge

### Unfelted Bone Gauge

24 sts and 36 rnds = 4" (10cm) in stockinette stitch on #2 (2.5mm or 2.75mm) needles, *or size to obtain correct gauge*

### Felted Bone Gauge

**note** Gauge is before felting

18 sts and 24 rnds = 4" (10cm) in stockinette stitch on #7 (4.5mm) needles or *size to obtain correct gauge*

### Unfelted Fetch Gauge

24 sts and 40 rnds = 4" (10cm) in Houndstooth Check patt on #2 (2.5mm or 2.75mm) needles, *or size to obtain correct gauge*

### Felted Fetch Gauge

**note** Gauge is before felting

18 sts and 24 rnds = 4" (10cm) in Houndstooth Check patt on #7 (4.5mm) needles, *or size to obtain correct gauge*

## Pattern Stitch

### Houndstooth Check Stitch

Worked over a multiple of 3 sts in the rnd.

**Rnd 1:** With Color B, k1, *sl1, k2, rep from * until last 2 sts, sl1, k1.

**Rnd 2:** With Color B, knit.

**Rnd 3** With Color C, * sl1, k2, rep from * until end of rnd.

**Rnd 4** With Color C, knit.

Repeat Rows 1–4 for Houndstooth Check stitch.

## Special Stitch Abbreviations

M1tbp—Make 1 through back of purl: inc 1 st by placing point of working (right-hand) needle behind other needle, inserting needle from the top through the purl st below next st, and knit; then knit the st above.

Kf&b—Inc by knitting in front and back of 1 st

## Instructions

**note** The first size listed is for the unfelted toy, worked on smaller needles. The second size is for the larger, felted toy, worked on larger needles. If there is only one set of instructions, it is meant for both size toys.

## Bone

With Color A and #2 (2.5mm or 2.75mm) for smaller, unfelted bone or #7 (4.5mm) dpns for larger, felted bone, CO 40 sts, evenly distributing sts on 3 dpns.

Join work and pm. Work 5 rnds even, knitting every rnd.

## Work Decreases

**Dec Rnd 1:** K8, k2tog, ssk, k16, k2tog, ssk, k8.

**Dec Rnd 2:** K7, k2tog, ssk, k14, k2tog, ssk, k7.

**Dec Rnd 3:** K6, k2tog, ssk, k12, k2tog, ssk, k6.

**Dec Rnd 4:** K5, k2tog, ssk, k10, k2tog, ssk, k5.

**Dec Rnd 5:** K4, k2tog, ssk, k8, k2tog, ssk, k4.

## Middle of the Bone

Work rem 20 sts even in St st for 4¾ (7)" (12.1 [17.8]cm) or until bone measures 6 (8½)" (15.2 [21.6]cm) in total length.

## Work Increases

**Inc Rnd 1:** K4, m1tbp, kf&b, k8, m1tbp, kf&b, k4.

**Inc Rnd 2:** K5, m1tbp, kf&b, k10, m1tbp, kf&b, k5.

**Inc Rnd 3:** K6, m1tbp, kf&b, k12, m1tbp, kf&b, k6.

**Inc Rnd 4:** K7, m1tbp, kf&b, k14, m1tbp, kf&b, k7.

**Inc Rnd 5:** K8, m1tbp, kf&b, k16, m1tbp, kf&b, k8—a total of 40 sts.

Work 5 rows even in St st. BO.

### Finishing

Weave in ends. With a tapestry needle, use mattress or whip st to sew one end securely.

### For smaller, unfelted bone:

Stuff firmly with old T-shirts or other cotton rags or wool roving or batting as desired. If using optional squeaker or bell, lodge this securely into the middle of the toy, taking care to surround it completely with stuffing.

Sew second end securely, reinforcing as necessary. Weave in ends deep inside of toy for safety's sake.

### For larger, felted bone:

Optional Embroidery:

With a tapestry needle and contrasting wool yarn, embroider your dog's name or another message, using the back st and forming the letters in a wide print that will still be readable when bone shrinks in the felting process.

**note** Avoid embroidery on unfelted bone, as the sts are likely to get caught on your dog's teeth.

Stuff loosely with old T-shirts or other cotton rags. Take care not to overstuff, as material will shrink in the felting process. If using optional squeaker or bell, lodge this securely into the middle of the toy, taking care to surround it completely with stuffing.

Sew second end securely.

To felt, put bone into washing machine with a pair of jeans or any other laundry that will tolerate a hot water wash and not create lint (avoid terry cloth towels).

Use the usual amount of detergent and a hot water, cold rinse wash cycle. Repeat as necessary to achieve the amount of felting you desire.

To dry the bone and increase felting, put in dryer briefly with laundry. Watch carefully to be sure the bone doesn't shrink too much. Lay flat on a towel, manipulating the bone into shape if necessary. It will take up to 2 days for the cotton stuffing to fully dry.

## Fetch

With Color B and size #2 (2.5mm or 2.75mm) for smaller, unfelted Fetch or #7 (4.5mm) dpns for larger, felted Fetch, CO 39 sts, evenly distributing sts on 3 dpns. Join and pm.

Knit 1 rnd with Color B.

Beg working Houndstooth Check patt. Rep Rnds 1–4 of patt until work measures 10 (12)" (25.4 [30.5cm]). End with Rnd 4.

Work 1 rnd with Color B.

BO.

## Finishing

Weave in ends. With a tapestry needle, use mattress or whip st to sew one end securely.

### For smaller, unfelted Fetch:

Stuff firmly with old T-shirts or other cotton rags or wool roving or batting as desired. If using optional squeaker or bell, lodge this securely into the middle of the toy, taking care to surround it completely with stuffing. Sew second end securely, reinforcing as necessary. Weave in ends deep inside of toy for safety's sake.

### For larger, felted Fetch:

Stuff loosely with old T-shirts or other cotton rags. Take care not to overstuff, as material will shrink in the felting process. If using optional squeaker or bell, lodge this securely into the middle of the toy, taking care to surround it completely with stuffing.

Sew second end securely.

To felt, put Fetch into washing machine with a pair of jeans or any other laundry that will tolerate a hot water wash and not create lint (avoid terry cloth towels).

Use the usual amount of detergent and a hot water, cold rinse wash cycle. Repeat as necessary to achieve the amount of felting you desire.

To dry Fetch and increase felting, put in dryer briefly with laundry. Watch carefully to be sure the Fetch doesn't shrink too much. Lay flat on a towel, manipulating the Fetch into shape if necessary. It will take up to 2 days for the cotton stuffing to fully dry.

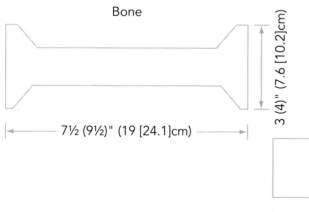

Bone

7½ (9½)" (19 [24.1]cm)

3 (4)" (7.6 [10.2]cm)

Fetch

11 (10½)" (27.9 [26.7]cm)

3½ (4½)" (8.9 [11.4]cm)

# Promoting Fair Trade and Fair Work

You may have heard about Fair Trade issues while buying a cup of coffee. Coffee is often labeled Fair Trade these days. When we define the details of "Fair Trade for Fair Work" for our food, we need the same understanding for our fibers. It's important to review how and where one's yarns were produced. Knitters in the industrialized world would not want to purchase yarn produced by child labor or other abusive practices—even if the yarn was inexpensive—that's an easy assumption. A more complicated issue comes in when we consider whether it's okay to purchase a low cost yarn that does support its workers in a place that has a lower cost of living. How much do we expect to contribute to workers in developing countries when we buy the fruits of their labors?

☙

Fair Trade or Fair Work is an issue that many people care about, although it's not always associated with yarn or even sustainability. Hanna Breetz, of the Green Knitter Web site, explains it this way, "The Fair Trade movement…promotes fair compensation for producers that have been historically marginalized, often with additional attention to gender equality, labor conditions, and environmental protection." Yet some environmentalists don't consider this movement to be part of their agenda. Breetz addresses this too, saying, "There's a strong argument to be made that a robust handicrafts or agricultural industry can give people the resources they need to protect their environment." Indeed, when people are paid fairly for their work and have reasonable work requirements, they often are able to devote energy to issues like education, health, the environment, and equality in ways they can't embrace while working in sweat shop conditions.

These issues often overlap with others mentioned in this book, particularly in chapter 4. You'll find that co-operatives, nonprofits, family-owned studios, and individuals who produce yarn and fiber are very likely considered to be Fair Trade establishments, or at the very least, follow some Fair Work tenets.

Issues concerning Fair Trade and Fair Work are often immediately associated with people who live in developing countries. While many wonderful and viable yarn companies with Fair Trade values may be working in South America, Asia, or Africa, these same principles can also be applied closer to home. The European Union does careful labeling to help consumers know where their purchases are made, but other countries, such as the United States, are not quite ready to insist on that level of accountability.

While we tend to be absorbed in development issues such as child labor, it's important

*Independent cooperatives can be found across the globe. Many utilize traditional skills and the unique cultural heritage of their region to provide a better standard of living for their communities. This knitter is a member of the La Imilla cooperative in Bolivia, which works with the KUSIKUY company in the U.S.*

to remember that many employees in United States fiber arts businesses may lack health insurance or are unable to earn a self-supporting wage. While it is an honor to work knitting or selling yarn, one should also be able to eat and pay the bills at the same time! Thus, when your local fiber farm or yarn shop boasts about a locally produced option but it seems too expensive for you to consider, remember that buying locally in the United States, such as supporting a co-operative like Green Mountain Spinnery or Tierra Wools, can also be a Fair Trade purchase.

There are many great options for those who want to purchase Fair Trade yarns that support women and children's issues, fair labor practices, and other Fair Work issues abroad. Here are just a few of those companies. Be sure to ask your local yarn store or favorite online source if you're looking for more ways to support Fair Trade and Fair Work initiatives through your knitting.

## Knit Picks: Affordable Yarns from Across the World

This mail-order and online retailer made its name by offering affordable yarns at low prices. Knit Picks' business model cut out the yarn company representatives, the distributors, and even the yarn shops in order to offer natural fiber yarns at a lower price. Now it shares this business model in common with many other online yarn retailers, but when Knit Picks began, its plan was innovative and new. Budget-minded knitters rejoiced and some in the yarn industry insisted the company must have been cutting corners

somewhere. The naysayers were convinced that this company wasn't valuing its workers if it was able to sell its yarns so inexpensively.

The truth? Knit Picks cares about its manufacturing partners—all over the world. In fact, its parent company, Crafts Americana, makes this statement: "Crafts Americana has very high standards for the International manufacturers we choose to work with. Executives from Crafts Americana have visited each of our manufacturers' factories personally to ensure that their facilities and labor practices are in line with both Crafts Americana's and our customers' expectations."

Specifically, Crafts Americana works only with manufacturers who...

- ∞ Institute management practices that respect the rights of all employees.
- ∞ Provide a safe and healthy work place.
- ∞ Promote the health and well-being of all employees.
- ∞ Oppose the use of child labor.
- ∞ Have an active role in the positive development of their local community.

Many companies make statements that can be hard to back up. However, I'm friendly with a colleague who works for Crafts Americana—and she sends me photos while she travels to factories. This company works with and inspects factories all over the world to be sure their employees are treated fairly and their products are up to snuff.

## Mango Moon: Recycling in Southeast Asia

Mango Moon's motto is "Doing Good, Having Fun." It's a fitting moniker as this Michigan business's most popular yarns are made from recycled saris, sarongs, and other Southeast Asian garments. Its sari silk and other recycled yarns are handspun into colorful novelty yarns that are genuinely fun. From an environmental standpoint, Mango Moon's sale of recycled fibers repurposed into knitting yarn is admirable. That, however, is just the beginning in terms of the "Doing Good" part of the motto.

All that spinning gets done as Mango Moon supports the nongovernmental organization Nepali Women Empowerment Group, which helps Nepali women rescued from abusive situations. Its Web site explains that, "the women who come to the shelter are able to use their spinning and knitting skills to rebuild their lives, while continuing to care for their children. Proceeds provide a safe shelter, healthcare, education, and the dignity of financial independence." Additional workers who contribute to making Mango Moon's yarn are part of a spinners' co-operative in Indonesia.

Mango Moon's line of colorful and "fun" yarns is growing, but its plan "to leave the world a little better than we found it" is the most admirable thing about it. Its plan is to "change the world one stitch at a time." It's an inspiring plan for knitters, don't you think?

## Mirasol Project: Supporting Traditional Textile Arts in Peru

Another Fair Trade yarn company that makes a difference is the Mirasol Project, in Peru. Their explanation says it best: "The Mirasol Project supports local communities in Peru through the sales of the Mirasol Yarn Collection. Peru's heritage and culture of textile artistry is rich and ancient. The Mirasol Yarn Collection includes yarn made from the animals tended by these communities for generations in the Peruvian highlands…. By purchasing it you are supporting the shepherds and their families ensuring the continuation of this tradition.

A portion of every purchase goes directly to the funding of a centre in the remote area of Munani in the region of Puno."

## Frog Tree Yarns: Creating Change in Bolivia and Peru

Frog Tree Yarns started purchasing products from Latin America in 1997. One of its primary products is alpaca yarn, produced by a Bolivian nonprofit co-operative. This nonprofit has trained somewhere between 800 to 1,200 women to knit this yarn, according to Frog Tree's Web site. The end result is employees who are fairly paid and can provide for their families and invest in developing their communities while maintaining traditional skills. The alpaca yarn has become so popular that Frog Tree is now working with a "socially conscious and environmentally friendly" group in Peru as well to produce more. Frog Tree itself is a not-for-profit company and any additional funds it earns after paying its artisans go to educational programs for both individuals and communities. Read more about Frog Tree yarns' Fair Trade initiatives at www.frogtreeyarns.com/FairTrade/tabid/61Default.aspx.

This chapter only mentions a few of the many wonderful companies who are making a difference when it comes to Fair Trade practices. Not only is it possible to support these initiatives by purchasing yarn, but the positive effects are also felt, stitch by stitch, when we mention these important activities to our knitter friends. We can choose to support environmentally conscious companies that include human beings within their plans for a positive impact on their ecosystem.

Tank Empire

# Tank Empire

The Directoire and Empire period in France and the Regency period in England left us the enduring and fabulous empire waist. The Tank Empire (Om-pier) draws on the clever fashion choices of that age. Loose folds, a high waist right under the bust, and natural fibers like cotton and linen offer supremely cool comfort in hot weather. When temperatures spike, a top like this can make all the difference while enjoying the summer sun. Knit in the round until the armholes, this pattern combines an interesting stitch pattern with a bit of color and a form fitting style. For those who live in colder climates, extend this long tank's season by wearing it over a skinny long sleeve shirt as a fashionable vest.

## Skill Level

Intermediate

## Size

This pattern looks best with several inches of negative ease.

Choose a size that offers up to 6" (15cm) of negative ease in fit. Sizes below fit up to the actual bust measurements given here. (Measure around widest area of bust for an accurate size.) For a looser fit, choose a size with finished measurements that allow for less negative ease.

34 (38, 41, 43, 46)" (86.4 [96.5, 104.1, 109.2, 116.8]cm)

## Finished Measurements

Bust: 28 (31½, 34½, 37, 40)" (71 [80, 87.6, 94, 101.6]cm)

## Materials

- Color A: 2 (2, 3, 3, 3) skeins of Knit Picks CotLin DK weight yarn, 70 percent Tanguis Cotton, 30 percent Linen, 123 yd. (112m), 1.75 oz. (50g), color 24139 Lantana
- Color B: 4 (4, 5, 6, 6) skeins of Knit Picks CotLin DK weight yarn, 70 percent Tanguis Cotton, 30 percent Linen, 123 yd. (112m), 1.75 oz. (50g), color 24467 Blackberry

or

- Color A: 246 (246, 369, 369, 369) yd. (224 [224, 336, 336, 336]m) of any DK weight yarn with the appropriate gauge
- Color B: 492 (492, 615, 738, 738) yd. (450 [450, 563, 675, 675]m) of any DK weight yarn with the appropriate gauge
- U.S. size 6 (4mm) circular needle, 32" (81cm) long, *or size to obtain gauge*
- U.S. size 5 (3.75mm) circular needle, 24" (61cm), *or size to obtain gauge*
- Stitch markers
- Stitch holder
- Tapestry needle
- U.S. size 5 (3.75mm) crochet hook

## Gauge

**note** A cotton/linen blend yarn will shrink when washed, especially after its first washing. It will stretch again in wearing, but note that the gauges for before and after washing differ. Measurements taken during knitting are based on the gauge before washing/blocking. Measurements on the schematic reflect the gauge after washing/blocking.

### Before washing/blocking:

19 sts and 26 rows = 4" (10cm) in Herringbone Stitch patt with larger needles

20 sts and 27 rows = 4" (10cm) in stockinette stitch with smaller needles

### After washing/blocking:

21 sts and 27 rows = 4" (10cm) in Herringbone Stitch patt with larger needles

21 sts and 28 rows = 4" (10cm) in stockinette stitch with smaller needles

## Pattern Stitches

### Special Stitch Abbreviation

M1tbp—Make 1 through back of purl: inc 1 st by placing point of working (right-hand) needle behind other needle, inserting needle from the top through the purl st below next st, and knit; then knit the st above.

### Herringbone Stitch Pattern

Worked over a multiple of 7 sts plus 1.

**Rnds 1 and 3:** Knit.

**Rnd 2:** *K2tog, k2, M1tbp, k2*, rep from * to *, end k1.

**Rnd 4:** K1, *k2, M1tbp, k2, k2tog, rep from *. Rep Rnds 1–4.

## Instructions

### Bottom of Tank/Empire Skirt

With Color A and a larger circular needle, CO 204 (232, 253, 274, 295) sts. Join and pm.

Work Herringbone Stitch patt in the rnd. Work two reps (8 rnds) in Color A.

Change color to Color B; work two reps (8 rnds) in Color B.

Continue, working above 16 rnds 4 (4, 5, 5, 6) times total, or until piece measures 10 (10, 12½, 12½, 15)" (25.4 [25.4, 31.8, 31.8, 38]cm). If you would prefer a shorter or cropped tank, work fewer reps of the Herringbone Stitch patt, as desired, but keep in mind that the skirt will shorten slightly when the finished garment is washed.

With Color A, work two reps (8 rnds). Cut yarn and join Color B.

### Shape Bust

With Color B, work dec as follows. Rnds 2 and 4 will each dec 29 (33, 36, 39, 42) sts per rnd.

**Rnds 1 and 3:** Knit.

**Rnd 2:** *K3tog, k1, M1tbp, k2*, rep from * to *, end with k1.

**Rnd 4:** K1, *k1, M1tbp, k1, k3tog rep from *

After this set of dec, you will have 146 (166, 181, 196, 211) sts on needle.

Knit 5 rnds. Pm at this point to facilitate measuring length of work later.

Change to a smaller circular needle.

Work even, knitting every rnd until St st measures 3½ (3½, 4, 4, 4½)" (9 [9, 10, 10, 11.4]cm) from marker.

## Divide for Back

The back and front will now be worked back and forth (knit 1 row, purl 1 row) in St st.

At rnd marker: BO 5 (5, 5, 5, 6) sts. Work 68 (78, 85, 93, 101) sts in St st.

Put rem 73 (83, 91, 98, 104) sts on st holder to be worked as front later.

Next dec row: BO 5 (5, 5, 5, 6) sts at the beg of the next row to create second armhole.

Work 1 row even.

Dec 1 st (by working k2tog or p2tog as relevant) at beg and end of row 2 (2, 2, 3, 3) times—59 (69, 76, 82, 89) sts.

Work even (knit 1 row, purl 1 row) until armhole measures 6½ (7, 7¼, 7¼, 7½)" 16.5 [17.8, 18.4, 18.4, 19]cm). End after WS row.

## Decrease for Back Neck

K20 (23, 26, 30, 33) for right back strap, BO 19 (23, 24, 26, 29) for neck, K20 (23, 26, 28, 30) sts for left back strap.

Put sts for right back strap on st holder.

## Left Back Strap

K2tog at beg of row at neck edge 3 (6, 7, 8, 8) times. Work even in St st on these 17 (17, 19, 20, 22) sts until armhole measures 8½ (9, 9½, 10, 10½)" (21.6 [22.9, 24.1, 25.4, 26.7]cm). BO.

## Right Back Strap

Attach matching yarn color to tank, work as Left Back Strap below, making matching decs at beg of row at neck edge.

## Tank Front

Put sts for Front back on smaller needle and join yarn.

BO 5 (5, 5, 5, 6) sts. Work 68 (78, 86, 93, 98) sts in St st.

**Next dec row:** BO 5 (5, 5, 5, 6) sts at the beg of the next row to create second armhole.

Work 1 row even.

Dec 1 st (by working k2tog or p2tog as relevant) at beg and end of row 2 (2, 2, 3, 3) times—59 (69, 77, 82, 86) sts.

Pm at last dec to facilitate measuring length of work later.

Work even (knit 1 row, purl 1 row) for 2¾ (3¼, 3½, 3¾, 4)" (7 [8.3, 8.9, 9.5, 10.2]cm) from marker. End after RS row.

## Tank V-Neck

Purl 28 (33, 37, 39, 41) sts. BO 3 (3, 3, 4, 4) sts pwise. Work rem 28 (33, 37, 39, 41) sts.

## Left Front V-Neck

Yarn is at outside edge of left front shoulder section. Work back and forth in St st, working p2tog at beg of each neck edge row 11 (16, 18, 19, 19) times until 17 (17, 19, 20, 22) sts rem.

Work even in St st until front matches back in length. BO.

## Right Front V-Neck

Put sts back on smaller needle and join yarn at neck edge. Work back and forth in St st, working p2tog at beg of each neck edge row 11 (16, 18, 19, 19) times until 17 (17, 19, 20, 22) sts rem.

Work even in St st until front matches back in length. BO.

## Finishing

Using a tapestry needle and matching yarn, sew shoulder seams with mattress st. Weave in ends.

With #5 (3.75mm) crochet hook and Color B yarn, work sc edging around armholes, neck edging, and bottom of tank. Weave in ends when finished with edging.

Block by hand washing or as appropriate for the yarn, according to the yarn label. Lay flat to dry.

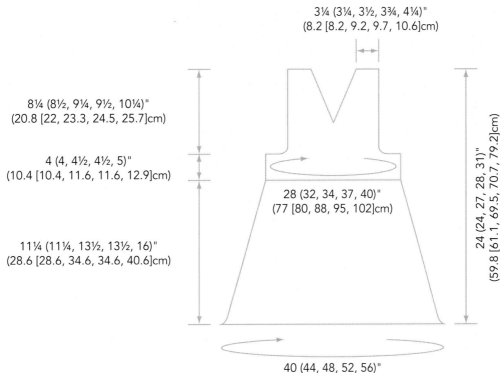

3¼ (3¼, 3½, 3¾, 4¼)"
(8.2 [8.2, 9.2, 9.7, 10.6]cm)

8¼ (8½, 9¼, 9½, 10¼)"
(20.8 [22, 23.3, 24.5, 25.7]cm)

4 (4, 4½, 4½, 5)"
(10.4 [10.4, 11.6, 11.6, 12.9]cm)

11¼ (11¼, 13½, 13½, 16)"
(28.6 [28.6, 34.6, 34.6, 40.6]cm)

28 (32, 34, 37, 40)"
(77 [80, 88, 95, 102]cm)

24 (24, 27, 28, 31)"
(59.8 [61.1, 69.5, 70.7, 79.2]cm)

40 (44, 48, 52, 56)"
(99 [112, 122, 133, 143]cm)

Sari Sack

# Sari Sack

Mango Moon yarns supports women and families in Nepal and Indonesia, providing safe shelter, healthcare, and education. That on its own would be a good reason to buy their yarn, but they're also using recycled silk as a material. What a great way to promote environmentalism! Now, once you've purchased some, what to do with those odd skeins of Sari silk that you couldn't resist? Make them into a fun and versatile simple bag, of course! This bag is knit with one strand of Mango Moon Recycled Silk and one strand of Dharma silk, knit together with a #10½ (6.5mm) circular needle to get a heavyweight material. The handspun Dharma silk adds a firm structure while the Recycled Sari Silk adds the color and style. The bag itself is simple—a stockinette stitch 12" (30.5cm)-tall drawstring sack with a flat base. Through an ingenious strap construction method, the bag can be worn over the shoulder, as a back pack, or across the chest as a messenger bag. The bag is a perfect size for those small essentials of a book, some sunscreen or makeup, sunglasses, and of course, one's knitting project. An optional lining is suggested for those who plan on stowing their keys and change in the bag as well.

## Skill Level

Easy

## Size

One size

## Finished Measurements

12" long × 10" wide (30.5 × 25.4cm)

Base is approximately 8" (20.3cm) wide

## Materials

**note** The fuzzy nature of Dharma's Recycled Silk yarn creates an I-cord strap that is very strong and a bit difficult to maneuver through the drawstring of this bag. This strength and texture is very good security if you plan to use this as a purse in an urban area; it's not easy to open or pull off your arm. However, if you prefer the convenience of a bag that opens easily, consider substituting a yarn with a smooth slick texture for the I-cord in this project.

- 2 skeins of Mango Moon Recycled Silk "Regular Weight" Sari yarn, 100 percent Silk, 150 yd. (137.2m), weights vary as this is a one-of-a-kind handspun yarn sold by length, varied multicolored

- 2 skeins of Mango Moon Dharma Solid Color Recycled Silk yarn, 100 percent Silk, 150 yd. (137.2m), weights vary as this is a one-of-a-kind handspun yarn sold by length, color 9406 Iris

or

- Combination of 300 yd. (274.3m) of any bulky weight and 300 yd. (274.3m) of any DK weight yarns that when knit together obtain appropriate gauge

or

- 600 yd. (549m) of any yarns that when knit together obtain appropriate gauge
- U.S. size 10½ (6.5mm) circular needle, 24" (61cm) long, or size to obtain gauge
- U.S. size 10½ (6.5mm) double-pointed needles, or size to obtain gauge
- Stitch markers
- Tapestry needle
- 13" × 25" (33cm × 63.5cm) rectangular piece of fabric for a lining (optional)
- Sewing thread and needle for a lining (optional)
- Iron (optional)

## Gauge

11 sts and 18 rows = 4" (10cm) over stockinette stitch with 1 strand each of Recycled Sari Silk and Dharma yarns

## Instructions

### Sack

Using a circular needle and 1 strand each of Recycled Sari Silk and Dharma, CO 70 sts. Join and pm. Work in St st (knit every row) for 12" (30.5cm).

### Work Drawstring Holes

K2, *k2tog, yo, rep from * until last 2 sts, k2. BO.

### Strap Loop

Using 2 dpns and 1 strand of Dharma yarn, CO 6 sts. Work St st I-cord for 6" (15.2cm). BO.

### Strap

Using 2 dpns and 1 strand of Dharma yarn, CO 6 sts. Work St st I-cord for 50" (127cm). BO.

### Finishing

Using a tapestry needle, weave in ends. If using silk for this bag, blocking is unnecessary.

With one strand of Dharma, sew closed CO edge on WS to make bag's bottom. With WS facing, flatten the beginning and end of the bottom seam so that each end makes a triangle. Measuring 2" (5cm) from each tip, sew a short seam to form an equilateral triangle on each end. (See Figure 1.)

Figure 1

Thread the I-cord through the drawstring holes, starting from the RS at the beginning of the eyelet row (in the middle of one of the wide sides of the bag), as shown in Figure 2. Thread the I-cord in and out of the holes, ending by threading the end from the WS through to the RS 4 sts from first end.

With RS facing, use a tapestry needle and 1 strand of Dharma silk to attach Strap loop at bottom of bag, directly below the I-cord Strap. Thread 1 end of strap through the loop, and sew the two ends of the strap together, reinforcing the join several times. (See Figure 2.)

**Optional Lining**

Fold fabric in half with RS facing. Using a needle and thread, use running st to sew up two sides. (See Figure 3.)

To make the bottom of the insert flat, iron bottom seam flat and create equilateral triangles as previously described for the Sack. (See Figure 4.)

Insert lining into knitted Sari Sack so that the WS of the lining is facing the WS of the Sari Sack. Fold over the edge of the lining fabric just underneath the drawstring area of the Sari Sack.

Using running st or whip st, sew the lining inside the bag, tucking under the unhemmed edge of the fabric to the WS to keep lining from fraying.

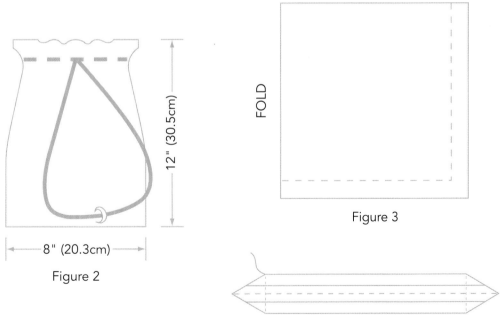

12" (30.5cm)

8" (20.3cm)

Figure 2

FOLD

Figure 3

Figure 4

# Scrubba Scrubba

Knit yourself an exfoliating mitt, washcloth, or soap satchel for your next shower or bath! This simple and quick project uses bast (plant) fibers like wild-grown nettle and cultivated hemp from Nepal, grown sustainably and handspun by local women. It travels a long way before knitting, if you don't live in Nepal, but it helps support small women's industries, maintains a traditional skill (hand spinning), and promotes the use of local foraging for nettle and sustainable crops such as hemp. These yarns may feel stiff and scratchy as you knit, but will soften over time and repeated use. Handspun can vary slightly in gauge from skein to skein, so gauge is approximate.

## Skill Level
Easy

## Size
Mitt fits a woman's medium hand

Soap Satchel and Washcloth are one size fits all

## Finished Measurements
Mitt, knitted with one strand each of nettle and hemp, is approximately 9" (22.9cm) long × 5½" (14cm) wide

Washcloth, knitted with two strands of yarn (the same type or mixed), is approximately 8" (20.3cm) long × 7" (17.8cm) wide

Soap Satchel, knitted with one strand of either yarn, is approximately 5" (12.7cm) long × 4" (10cm) wide

## Materials
**note** The handspun hemp and nettle yarns come in balls or skeins of varying weights and lengths, usually a weight of between 3–3½ oz. (95–100g) and between 150–250 yd. (140–230m). You need two balls or skeins to make this whole set of projects, and can mix or match the yarns, as available or desired.

- 1 skein of Himalaya Yarns Nepalese Handspun Nettle (Aloo) yarn, 100 percent Nettle, 205 yd. (187m), 3½ oz. (100g), natural color
- 1 skein of Himalaya Yarns Nepalese Handspun Hemp Yarn, 100 percent Hemp, 205 yd. (187m), 3½ oz. (100g), natural color

or

- 410 yd. (374m) of any bast (plant) fiber yarn with the appropriate gauge
- U.S. size 8 (5mm) straight needles or circular needle, *or size to obtain gauge*
- U.S. size 4 (3.5mm) double-pointed needles
- Stitch marker
- Tapestry needle
- Soap (optional)

## Gauge

### Mitt Gauge

11 sts and 15 rows = 4" (10cm) in garter stitch with one strand of each yarn knit together on size 8 (5mm) needles

### Washcloth Gauge

11 sts and 21 rows = 4" (10cm) in stockinette stitch with two strands of yarn or one strand each of nettle and hemp on #8 (5mm) needles

### Soap Satchel Gauge

20 sts and 30 rows = 4" (10cm) in stockinette stitch with one strand of yarn, on #4 (3.5mm) dpns

## Instructions

**note** For all three designs below, to create a neat edge, at the last st of each plain-knit row, wyif, sl1 pwise.

### Mitt

**note** This mitt is knit flat and then stitched up afterward.

With #8 (5mm) needles and one strand each of Nettle and Hemp yarns, CO 30 sts.

Work in garter st, knitting every row, until piece measures 9" (23cm) or desired length.

### Shape Top

**Row 1:** K2tog, k10, k2tog, k2, k2tog, k10, k2tog.

**Row 2:** K2tog, k8, k2tog, k2, k2tog, k8, k2tog.

**Row 3:** K2tog, k6, k2tog, k2, k2tog, k6, k2tog.

BO rem 18 sts.

### Make I-Cord Loop

Using one strand of either yarn, CO 6 sts with a #4 (3.5mm) dpn. Work I-cord for 4" (10cm).

BO as follows: *K2tog, k1, BO, rep once from *. BO last 2 sts by passing first st over second, cut tail of yarn and pull through last st.

### Finishing

Weave in ends.

Fold in half and use a tapestry needle and one strand of yarn to sew up mitt. Starting at the CO edge, stitch up 4" (10cm). Leave a 2" (5cm) hole, making sure to reinforce sts before and after thumb hole. (Adjust placement of thumb hole to fit your hand if necessary.) Continue stitching up and across top of mitt.

Using a tapestry needle, sew ends of I-cord firmly to the opposite side of the mitt from the thumb hole, to create a loop to hang up the mitt to dry.

### Washcloth

With #8 (5mm) needles and 2 strands of yarn, CO 22 sts.

Knit 2 rows.

Work in St st until piece measures 6½" (16.5cm), ending after knit row.
Knit 1 row.

BO.

Make I-cord as for mitt.

### Finishing

Weave in ends.

Using a tapestry needle, sew ends of I-cord firmly to one corner of the washcloth, to create a loop to hang up the washcloth to dry.

### Soap Satchel

With #4 (3.5mm) dpns and one strand of yarn, CO 44 sts. Join to work in the round and pm. Work St st (knit every rnd) until piece measures 4½" (11.4cm) or roughly ½" (1.3cm) longer than your bar of soap.

## Make Drawstring Holes

Beg at marker, *k5 sts, yo, k2tog, rep from * to last 2 sts, end with k2.

Knit 3 rnds.

BO.

## Drawstring

Make I-cord as previously described, working I-cord until it measures 10" (25.5cm). BO as above.

## Finishing

Weave in ends.

With a tapestry needle and matching yarn, use a running st at CO edge of satchel. Pull it tight to close up the bottom. Tie this off by adding a couple of extra sts to make sure the bottom is securely fastened.

Work drawstring through eyelets created at the top of the bag. Tie a knot in the drawstring so the bag can be hung up in the shower or bath. Put your preferred soap into the satchel and enjoy!

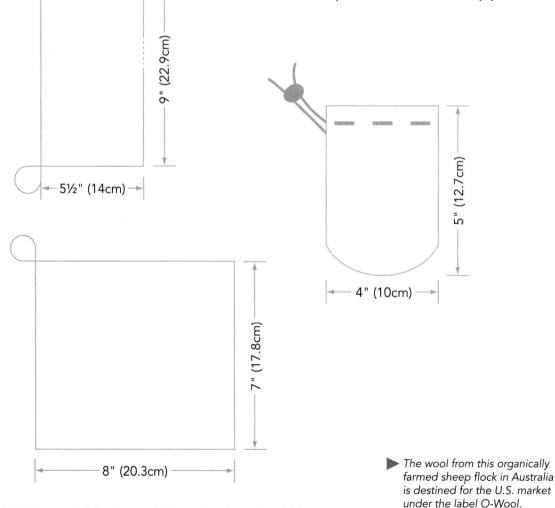

9" (22.9cm)

5½" (14cm)

7" (17.8cm)

8" (20.3cm)

5" (12.7cm)

4" (10cm)

▶ *The wool from this organically farmed sheep flock in Australia is destined for the U.S. market under the label O-Wool.*

# Organic and Natural Fibers and Labeling Use

Whether you go to the grocery store or your yarn shop, the array of labels and claims on products for sale can be dizzying. It's confusing while shopping for food—free-range, organic, naturally grown, locally grown—and it can be even more baffling at the yarn shop. If you're like me, the terms bandied about can become overwhelming, especially when I'm short on time. Ever stand in the grocery store in front of the eggs, wondering which free-range, organic, vegetarian feed, cage-free dozen is the right carton to buy?

Yarn shop labels say "natural," "eco-wool," "organic," and a variety of other things to catch your attention. For some consumers, any attempt at labeling green fibers processing is valued, but for others, the specifics are crucial. Knitters with chemical sensitivities or allergies must be sure their knitting yarn is safe; otherwise, they risk hives, rashes, or even problems breathing from their latest yarn purchase! Those knitting for newborns and small children want to swathe their cherished children in handmade clothing without exposing them to pesticides. How do we know what to choose? What does the term "organic" mean? What about all the other terms?

*Organic* is a legal word used in agricultural certification. That legal definition means certification may differ slightly from country to country. While there are differences between certifying agencies, many of the underlying values are similar. Although the United States is just one country with an organic program and by no means the strictest, I'll refer to it here as an example. It's called the National Organic Program (NOP).

First, the United States Department of Agriculture designates two categories of organic labeling as it refers to yarn. The first relates to raw natural fibers, such as cotton, wool, or flax. These agricultural products "are covered under the NOP/livestock production standards." This first set of standards refers to whether the fiber or fiber-producing animal has been grown organically. It doesn't indicate anything about how the fiber has been treated after it leaves the farm.

The second category is "Labeling for Certified Handling/Processing/Manufacturing Operations." This designation applies to how organic fiber is treated after it leaves the farm; in this case, the washing, carding, spinning, and processing of that fiber into yarn. One cannot seek certification for organic fiber processing unless the fiber itself is certified organic in the first place.

The two examples I use below, wool and cotton, are by no means the only natural fibers available for organic certification. In fact, all natural fibers could potentially be available in a legally organic form. However, these are two common fibers for knitting yarns, so I've started with the basics.

## Using Organic Wool

Let's use the example of livestock certification for wool, a fiber we knitters know well. For a farm's sheep to be certified organic, the animals must be fed only organic grain and organic pasture forage. No synthetic hormones, vaccines, or genetic engineering are allowed. No pesticides can be fed to the sheep, put on the sheep, or on the pastures. Finally, the farmer must boost livestock health through maintaining good management practices and sustaining the farm's ecosystem. (This means rotating the grazing so that the sheep don't do harm to the fields through overgrazing, etc.)

Organic management of sheep allows a farmer to manage pests and parasites without chemicals through the use of improved nutrition, pasture maintenance, and the isolation and treatment of sick animals. All this care allows the wool to be certified organic as *only* a raw material. It can't be labeled 100 percent organic or organic unless the processing of the fiber into yarn is also certified organic under the "Labeling for Certified Handling/Processing/Manufacturing Operations." However, there is a loop hole. The National Organic Program in the United States "does not restrict the use of the term 'made with organic…'" So, if a textile product has a minimum of 70 percent certified organic fibers, it can be labeled "made with organic…" but this doesn't guarantee any kind of organic processing. Also, this choice doesn't allow the use of the USDA Organic seal.

Where does this leave consumers who seek organic wool? There aren't many producers of certified organic wool in the United States. That's because, in part, there aren't many sheep producers in the United States in the first place! However, even among sheep producers, very few can manage the switch to an entirely organic operation. Sheep parasites are a serious issue in many areas of the United States simply because of the

▲ *More choices for organic cotton have sprung up in recent years.*

temperate weather conditions. It can be hard (though not impossible) to kill off worms, lice, flies, and other pests that cause problems for sheep in humid, hot conditions, particularly if one's climate doesn't get cold enough for a sustained hard freeze. Small scale farmers in the United States may have access to organic pastures but not to organic feed grain, which is often in short supply. Finally, some small farmers may run a nearly organic operation but lack the funds or wherewithal to undertake the certification process.

As a result of the limited wool production and difficulties involved with organic certification, many of the organic yarns available in the United States use certified organic wool that is imported from other countries. While this maintains the purity of the organic certification in legal terms, the cost of importation is in the amount of petroleum used to transport a big, bulky product like wool across the world. Environmentally, organic wool is a great idea—but the fuel costs and resultant pollution of getting it to your local yarn store might be prohibitive.

## Using Organic Cotton

In previous chapters, I've mentioned information about organic cotton. The previously mentioned NOP regulations concerning organic fiber growth and labeling, processing, and manufacturing apply to cotton, too. Cotton is a crop that is heavily dependent on pesticides and fertilizers in the United States, and any efforts toward sustainable cotton production are a good thing for the environment and for our health. Cotton is a fiber we all wear, knit, and use in our daily lives, yet most of us don't pursue its origins carefully. Ideally, an effort to refocus our purchases and concerns about organic yarns would extend to ready-made clothing as well, and this is one issue that makes a big difference.

Studies show that people absorb chemicals (pesticides, carcinogens, etc.) through the skin. New mothers are usually the first to focus on organic cottons for their babies. If you do this, bear in mind the two steps in organic certification mentioned earlier in this chapter. Not only does the cotton need to be grown organically, but it needs to be processed organically—and this includes the removal of dirt and wax in washing, the dyeing process, and the oils used in spinning cotton. There are a lot of chances to be exposed to potential allergens and irritants long after the cotton is harvested from the field. For instance, mercerization of cotton makes the cotton look shiny and changes the hand of a knitting yarn. It's a tempting product, but one

that is created through a gassing process…and it's not organic! In this case, it's the processing that matters—always investigate before assuming that because it's made from organic cotton, it's also processed that way. It's to everyone's advantage to support increased organic cotton production, from boll to onesie or from boll to yarn skein. A great way to reduce risk at this point is to find a yarn which not only says it's organic, but also has the certification information on the label.

An organic certification has to come from a legal certifying agency. Some yarn labels go as far as to mention the certifying agency, whereas others will list it on their Web site. For instance, Green Mountain Spinnery's organic wool yarns indicate that the wool is certified organic and that the processing is certified by the Vermont Organic Farmers as a part of the NOP. Their Cotton Comfort line uses fine wool (not certified organic) and 20 percent organic cotton. While their processing for this yarn may not be organic, the cotton used is organic U.S. cotton. Its custom yarn processing (for farmers who wish to produce their own yarns) indicates clearly how much it costs, per pound, to use certified organic processing as compared to their regular processing. In Green Mountain Spinnery's case, even its "regular" processing is intended to be as sustainable and green as possible—but not everyone's is.

An example of a widely available certified organic 100% cotton yarn, Lion Organic Cotton, is grown in Peru in several natural colors. According to Lion Brand's information, "Using appropriate technologies and fair trade practices, Lion Organic Cotton is converted from field to yarn with sustainable processing, certified by the Dutch foundation, SKAL, owner of the prestigious EKO quality symbol."

Despite the fact that the United States is the world's second largest cotton grower, at this point, organic cotton is much more likely to come from India, China, or a variety of countries in South America and Africa. It's hard to comprehend the scale at which chemically intensive cotton growing has taken over in the last 50 or so years. That said, since the 1990s, designers in the fashion world have advocated for increased amounts of organic cotton, and slowly, more is being grown and made available. It's possible to buy organic cotton yarn that is grown and processed in the United States. One such yarn is Hope USA cotton, a double knitting weight yarn, produced by Kollage. Buying an organic yarn that is locally produced both reduces one's carbon footprint through transportation and through the choice of organically grown and produced fiber.

## What Does "Transitional" Mean?

Many farmers plan to convert their crops or livestock to become certified organic. Yarn companies, too, sometimes work toward organic certification. However, this takes time…in most cases, several years. During this time, you may hear that a small wool producer, for instance, is "transitional." This means that while he or she is slowly working to become an organic producer, this farmer isn't yet eligible for organic certification. This isn't a bad label—it means that this producer is working in the right direction to promote sustainability! It's worth supporting farmers in these categories, but if you have allergies or other sensitivities, do consider investigating further.

A farmer or yarn company who is truly working toward producing an organic product shouldn't be upset to answer your questions. Ask if their animals or fields are treated with pesticides or petrochemical fertilizers. Ask if their sheep are dipped (immersed in chemicals to reduce parasites) or wormed. In some cases, organic grain isn't available for sheep, and hence, the wool can't be called organic yet even if everything else is acceptable.

Finding out more information shouldn't feel difficult or uncomfortable. In my experience, farmers and yarn companies who convert to an organic product are bright, thoughtful, and excited about their plans for the future. Be wary if, when you ask politely, the producer doesn't want to volunteer information about what this transitional status means to you, the consumer.

## What About All Those Other Terms?

Sadly, the only way to create a consistent labeling process is to legislate it. While the European Union has created a more comprehensive labeling process than the United States, the one thing that's universal is the use of confusing words that may not mean much. Here are some of the terms you may hear. Without actually following up with further research, there is no guarantee that these labels are anything more than marketing terms.

- **Natural:** This is a term that has popped onto all sorts of packaging. It may be true, but there's often no way to tell on one's own. One exception is the use of the term "natural colored" wool/cotton/Angora, etc. Fibers come in a startling array of natural shades, often orchestrated by careful breeding or blending of fibers. Natural-color wools will be shades of brown, black, tan, white, and gray…some fibers may appear reddish or blue and still be natural colors. Natural-color cottons are usually variations of green, brown, orange, and white. Essentially, natural color means the fiber hasn't been dyed.

- **Green Cotton:** There are no federal guidelines in the United States to indicate what this term means…and I've looked far and wide! It doesn't mean organic-certified fiber. Apparently, there is some indication that "green cotton" shouldn't have been bleached or treated with formaldehyde in its processing. However, there's no way to guarantee the processing avoids these chemicals, as there is no certification process. Look with skepticism on any advertising that indicates "eco-friendly" with no details about how the land is being protected from pesticides or fertilizations, how water usage is being reduced, or how the fiber itself is being treated.

- **Low-Impact Dyes:** This means the dyes used in coloring the fiber are intended to have less of an impact on the environment than conventional dyes. This might mean the synthetic dyes used are less environmentally dangerous or less water is used in the dyeing process. However, this term isn't legislated, and there's no certifying agency to determine that the company actually uses these practices. It's worth researching further if you're interested in a specific claim of low-impact dyes.

- **Natural Dyes:** Natural dyeing indicates that the dyes are made from botanically derived materials. This largely means plant matter, although cochineal, a red dye, comes from an insect. Natural dyeing produces rich and complex colors, but the dyeing process itself doesn't necessarily end up being more environmentally friendly. The person who harvests the dye plants must grow and harvest them sustainably, particularly if they are found in the wild. The dyes must be used safely, with mordants that won't pollute the water supply or endanger the dyer or others. (*Mordants* are chemicals used to ensure the dyes "stick" to the fibers, such as alum, copper, tin, lead, and other chemicals.) How the exhausted dye bath and the plant fibers are disposed of is also a concern. Natural dyeing processes don't use synthetic (petroleum-based) products but don't automatically conserve water or necessarily protect the environment either.

- **Eco-Friendly:** At first glance, ecologically friendly seems like a great term! It means that the person who uses it thinks about environmental issues. Unfortunately, the details and definition are where all the facts are made clear—and sometimes, marketing copy can be very slick. Eco-friendly won't assure the consumer much of anything because it lacks a specific definition. It doesn't necessarily mean that the fiber is organic, the processing is sensitive to environmental concerns, or even that the packaging is made from recycled materials. It means only what it says, "Ecologically Friendly." Some companies use this term in good faith, but you'll have to pursue it to figure out what, exactly, they mean when they tell you they care about an ecosystem.

Pixie Mitts

# Pixie Mitts

Knit your favorite pixie a set of mittens! Keeping warm in cold climates requires everybody to wear mittens, even those of us with whimsy on our minds. This design includes multiple sizes to spice up wintertime blues and add variety to our mitten wear. Wool stays warm when wet and when raised organically, is a fabulous renewable resource. Worsted weight wool and a pattern only at the tip of the mitten and thumb makes this a quick but stimulating project...perfect for matching mom and kid mittens!

## Skill Level

Intermediate

## Size

4 Years (6 Years, 8 Years, Woman's Small, Woman's Large)

## Finished Measurements

Hand circumference: 6 (6½, 7, 7½, 8)" (15.2 [16.5, 17.8, 19.1, 20.3]cm)

## Materials

Samples knit in:

- 1 skein of Lorna's Laces Green Line Worsted weight yarn, 100 percent organic Merino wool, 210 yd. (192m), 4 oz. (113.4g), color Growth (green), Dusk (purple), Mirth (pink), Solitude (gold), Courage (red-orange)

or

- 210 yd. (192m) of any worsted weight yarn with the appropriate gauge
- U.S. size 5 (3.75mm) double-pointed needles, *or size to obtain gauge*
- U.S. size 8 (5mm) double-pointed needles, *or size to obtain gauge*
- 3 stitch markers
- Row counter
- Stitch holder or safety pin
- Tapestry needle

## Gauge

18 sts and 24 rows = 4" (10cm) in stockinette stitch

**note** Check row gauge; correct row gauge will affect the sizing of this pattern. If your row gauge is different, and with this yarn it did vary from one knitter to another, adjustment points are noted in the pattern.

## Instructions

### Mitten Cuff

With #5 dpns, CO 26 (28, 30, 32, 34) sts. Join and pm.

Work in k1, p1 rib until the work measures 2¾" (7 cm).

Next Rnd: With size #8 dpns, knit, increasing 2 sts evenly distributed across rnd—28 (30, 32, 34, 36) sts.

Work 4 rnds of St st. (Knit every rnd.)

### Shape Thumb Gusset

Set up gusset: Beg at marker, K13 (14, 15, 16, 17). Pm. Inc 1 in each of next 2 sts. Pm. Knit until end of rnd.

Rnd 1: Knit.

Rnd 2: K13 (14, 15, 16, 17), inc 1 st after first marker, knit thumb sts, inc 1 st before second marker. Knit until end of rnd.

Rep Rnds 1 and 2, increasing inside markers to create thumb until there are 12 (12, 14, 14, 16) sts between markers.

Next Rnd: K14 (15, 16, 17, 18) sts, removing first marker and working first st of gusset. Put 10 (10, 12, 12, 14) sts on small stitch holder or safety pin to be worked later. Knit until end of rnd, leaving rem marker in place to denote beg of rnd—28 (30, 32, 34, 36) sts.

### Work Hand

Work even, knitting every rnd, until St st measures 2 (2½ ,3, 3½, 4)" (5.1 [6.4, 7.6, 8.9, 10.2]cm) or mitten is 3" (7.6cm) shorter than desired length.

### Work Pixie Texture

Rnd 1: *K1, p1, rep from *.

Rnd 2: Purl.

Rnd 3: *K1, p1, rep from *.

Rnd 4: Knit.

Rnd 5: *P1, k1, rep from *.

Rnd 6: Purl.

Rnd 7: *P1, k1, rep from *.

Rnd 8: Knit.

Rnds 9–11: Rep Rnds 1–3.

### For Woman's Small (Large) Only:

Dec 2 (4) sts evenly placed across Rnd 12, for a total of 32 sts.

Rnd 12: Knit.

Not including ribbing, mitten should measure 4 (4½, 5, 5½, 6)" (10 [11.5, 12.5, 14, 15]cm) at this point. If it is not yet this length, add additional St st rnds at this point.

### Shape Pixie Mitt Spiral Decrease

For Size 4 Years (on 28 sts):

Rnd 1: *K5, sl1 kwise, p1, psso, rep from * until end of rnd.

Rnd 2: K5, sl1 kwise, p1, psso, *k4, sl1 kwise, p1, psso, rep from *, end k4, sl1 kwise.

Rnd 3: P1, psso, k4, sl1 kwise, p1, psso, *k3, sl1 kwise, p1, psso, rep from *, end k3.

Rnd 4: Sl1 kwise, p1, psso, k3, sl1 kwise, p1, psso, *k2, sl1 kwise, p1, psso, rep from *, end k2.

Rnd 5: Sl1 kwise, p1, psso, k2, sl1 kwise, p1, psso, *k1, sl1 kwise, p1, psso, rep from * end k1.

Rnd 6: Sl1 kwise, p1, psso, k1, *sl1 kwise, p1, psso, rep from *.

**Rnd 7:** *Sl1 kwise, p1, psso, rep from *, end k1, for a total of 3 sts on dpns.

### For Size 6 Years (on 30 sts):

**Rnd 1:** *K4, sl1 kwise, p1, psso, rep from * until end of rnd.

**Rnd 2:** K4, sl1 kwise, p1, psso, *k3, sl1 kwise, p1, psso, rep from *, end k3, sl1 kwise.

**Rnd 3:** P1, psso, k3, sl1 kwise, p1, psso, *k2, sl1 kwise, p1, psso, rep from *, end k2.

**Rnd 4:** Sl1 kwise, p1, psso, k2, sl1 kwise, p1, psso, *k1, sl1 kwise, p1, psso, rep from *, end k1.

**Rnd 5:** Sl1 kwise, p1, psso, k1, sl1 kwise, p1, psso, * sl1 kwise, p1, psso, rep from *.

**Rnd 6:** *Sl1 kwise, p1, psso, rep from * until 3 sts on dpns.

### For Sizes 8 Years, Woman's Small, and Woman's Large (on 32 sts):

**Rnd 1:** *K6, sl1 kwise, p1, psso, rep from * until end of rnd.

**Rnd 2:** K6, sl1 kwise, p1, psso. *K5 sts, sl1 kwise, p1, psso, rep from *, end k5, sl1 kwise.

**Rnd 3:** P1, psso, k5, sl1 kwise, p1, psso, *k4, sl1 kwise, p1, psso, rep from *, end k4.

**Rnd 4:** Sl1 kwise, p1, psso, k4, sl1 kwise, p1, psso, *k3, sl1 kwise, p1, psso, rep from *, end k3.

**Rnd 5:** Sl1 kwise, p1, psso, k3, sl1 kwise, p1, psso, *k2, sl1 kwise, p1, psso, rep from *, end k2.

**Rnd 6:** Sl1 kwise, p1, psso, k2, sl1 kwise, p1, psso, *k1, sl1 kwise, p1, psso, rep from *, end k1.

**Rnd 7:** Sl1 kwise, p1, psso, k1, * sl1 kwise, p1, psso, rep from *.

**Rnd 8:** *Sl1 kwise, p1, psso, rep from * end k1 for a total of 3 sts on dpns.

### For All Sizes:

Transfer 3 rem sts to 1 #8 (5mm) dpn.

On rem 3 sts, knit I-cord for 1½" (4cm).

K1, k2tog, BO.

Tie knot in I-cord.

## Make Thumb

With #8 (5mm) dpns, pick up 10 (10, 12, 12, 14) sts from holder and pick up and knit 2 sts over gap for a total of 12 (12, 14, 14, 16) sts on needles. Join and pm.

Work Pixie Texture Rnds 1–8 to match the mitten's palm texture.

### Shape Thumb Top for Sizes 4 Years and 6 Years (on 12 sts):

**Rnd 1:** *K1, sl1 kwise, p1, psso, rep from *.

**Rnd 2:** K1, sl1 kwise, p1, psso. *Sl1 kwise, p1, psso, rep from *, end k1.

**Rnd 3:** K1, sl1 kwise, p1, psso. Sl1 kwise, p1, psso.

On rem 3 sts, knit I-cord for 1½" (4cm).

K1, k2tog, BO.

Tie knot in I-cord.

### Shape Thumb Top for Sizes 8 Years and Woman's Small (on 14 sts):

**Rnd 1:** *K2, sl1 kwise, p1, psso, rep from *, end k2.

**Rnd 2:** K2, sl1 kwise, p1, psso, *k1, sl1 kwise, p1, psso, rep from *, end k1.

**Rnd 3:** K2, sl1 kwise, p1, psso, *sl1 kwise, p1, psso, rep from *.

**Rnd 4:** K2, *sl1 kwise, p1, psso, rep from *, end k1.

On rem 3 sts, knit I-cord for 1½" (4cm).

K1, k2tog, BO.

Tie knot in I-cord.

### Shape Thumb Top for Size Women's Large (on 16 sts):

**Rnd 1:** *K2, sl1 kwise, p1, psso, rep from *.

**Rnd 2:** K2, sl1 kwise, p1, psso, *k1, sl1 kwise, p1, psso, rep from *, end k2.

**Rnd 3:** K2, sl1 kwise, p1, psso, *sl1 kwise, p1, psso, rep from *, end k1.

**Rnd 4:** K2, * sl1 kwise, p1, psso, rep from *.

**Rnd 5:** K2, sl1 kwise, p1, psso.

On rem 3 sts, knit I-cord for 1½" (4cm).

K1, k2tog, BO.

Tie knot in I-cord.

## Finishing

Weave in ends, closing any stitch gaps around thumb. Wash gently and lay flat to block.

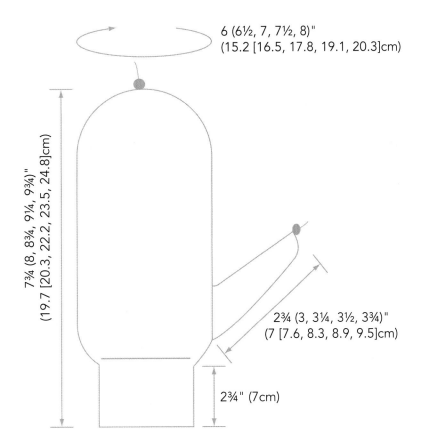

6 (6½, 7, 7½, 8)"
(15.2 [16.5, 17.8, 19.1, 20.3]cm)

7¾ (8, 8¾, 9¼, 9¾)"
(19.7 [20.3, 22.2, 23.5, 24.8]cm)

2¾ (3, 3¼, 3½, 3¾)"
(7 [7.6, 8.3, 8.9, 9.5]cm)

2¾" (7cm)

# Spire Smock

Organic wool can be everything you dream of in a knitting yarn—and more! The same is true for this sweater. While keeping warm, you can look fashionable and sophisticated as well. The Spire Smock's knit in an interesting twisted stitch pattern, with careful details to accentuate your waist and a dynamite neckline that brings attention to one's face. Why is it called Spire Smock? This stitch pattern, originally called "Fractured Lattice" by Barbara Walker in her book, *A Second Treasury of Knitting Patterns* (Scribner's, 1970) reminds me of the skyline of a medieval city, full of spires…so I have transformed it into the spires of my imagination. With its three quarter length sleeves, wide collar, and single button closure, it might remind you of a painter's smock with much more ornate appeal.

## Skill Level
Intermediate

## Size
S (M, L)

## Finished Measurements
Bust: 35" (41½, 48)"
(88.9 [105.4, 121.9]cm)

## Materials
- 7 (7, 8) skeins of O-wool Classic yarn, 100 percent Certified Organic Merino wool, 198 yd. (181m), 3½ oz. (100g), color 6402 Saffron

or

- 1386 (1386, 1584) yd. (1,267.4 [1,267.4, 1,448.4]m) of any worsted weight yarn with the appropriate gauge
- U.S. size 5 (3.75mm) circular needle, 24" (61cm) long, *or size to obtain gauge*
- Stitch markers
- 3 stitch holders
- Row counter
- Safety pin or other marker
- Tapestry needle
- 1 button, 1" (25mm) to 1⅛" (29mm) diameter (see sidebar)
- 1 smaller button—approximately ¾" (19mm) to anchor larger button, above, on sweater's WS
- Sewing needle and matching thread

## Gauge

**note** The ribbing is flexible. It will contract at the edges of the garment, and can be blocked out to larger dimensions on the sleeves and collar, which end up at about 23 sts = 4" (10cm).

26 sts and 26 rows = 4" (10cm) in 1 × 1 ribbing

20 sts and 26 rows = 4" (10cm) in Spire stitch

## Pattern Stitches

### Special Stitch Abbreviations

**Right Twist (RT):** k2tog, leaving sts on (left) needle, insert (right) needle from the front in between 2 sts just worked and knit first st again, slip both sts off needle.

**Left Twist (LT):** Skip 1 st, knit second st through back loop but do not slip off (left) needle, knit first and second st together through back loop.

**Make 1 through back of purl (M1tbp):** inc 1 st by placing point of working (right hand) needle behind other needle, inserting needle from the top through the purl st below next st, and knit; then knit the st above.

**Purl in front and back (pf&b):** Purl 1 in front and back of st to work 1 st inc.

**SSP:** Slip 2 sts singly as if to knit; move them back to the left needle. Insert right needle through back loops of the slipped sts and purl them together.

### 1 × 1 Ribbing #1

**Row 1 (WS):** *P1, k1; rep from *.

**Row 2:** Knit the knit sts and purl the purl sts.

Rep Rows 1 and 2 to form 1 × 1 ribbing.

### 1 × 1 Ribbing #2

**Row 1 (WS):** *K1, p1; rep from *.

**Row 2:** Knit the knit sts and purl the purl sts.

Rep Rows 1 and 2 to form 1 × 1 ribbing.

### Spire Pattern

Worked over a multiple of 8 sts.

**Row 1, 3, 5, and 7 (WS):** Purl.

**Row 2:** *LT, k2, LT, RT, rep from *.

**Row 4:** K1, *LT, k2, RT, k2; rep from *, ending last rep k1.

**Row 6:** *RT, LT, RT, k2; rep from *.

**Row 8:** K3, *LT, k2, RT, k2, rep from * to last 5 sts, end LT, k3.

Rep Rows 1–8.

## Instructions

### Back

CO 92 (108, 124) sts.

Set up patt as follows (WS): Work edging of 1 × 1 Ribbing #1 for 10 sts. Pm. Work Row 1 of Spire patt until last 10 sts. Pm. Work edging of 1 × 1 Ribbing #2 for 10 sts.

Cont, working 10 sts of 1 × 1 ribbing as established before marker, working 9 (11, 13) reps of Spire patt between markers, and working 1 × 1 ribbing as established after marker until work measures approximately 5 (6, 7½)" (12.7 [15.2, 19.1]cm) or until 2.5" (6.4cm) before reaching desired waistline. End after Row 8 of Spire patt; for average sizing, this will be after 4 (5, 6) reps of Rows 1–8.

## Waist Shaping

Work 4 reps of Rows 1–8 of Spire patt as follows. The even-numbered rows are worked exactly as established, while waist shaping takes place within the 1 × 1 ribbing panels on the odd-numbered (WS) rows. The first 2 reps dec edging to define waist while the second 2 reps inc edging toward the bust. Throughout shaping, maintain 1 × 1 ribbing patt along each edge as previously established.

### Decrease Rows

**Row 1:** Work 8 sts of 1 × 1 ribbing, p2tog before marker, purl until next marker, ssp, work last 8 sts in 1 × 1 ribbing.

**Row 3:** Work 7 sts of 1 × 1 ribbing, p2tog before marker, purl until next marker, ssp, work last 7 sts in 1 × 1 ribbing.

**Row 5:** Work 6 sts of 1 × 1 ribbing, p2tog before marker, purl until next marker, ssp, work last 6 sts in 1 × 1 ribbing.

**Row 7:** Work 5 sts of 1 × 1 ribbing, p2tog before marker, purl until next marker, ssp, work last 5 sts in 1 × 1 ribbing.

**Row 1:** Work 4 sts of 1 × 1 ribbing, p2tog before marker, purl until next marker, ssp, work last 4 sts in 1 × 1 ribbing.

**Row 3:** Work 3 sts of 1 × 1 ribbing, p2tog before marker, purl until next marker, ssp, work last 3 sts in 1 × 1 ribbing.

**Row 5:** Work 2 sts of 1 × 1 ribbing, p2tog before marker, purl until next marker, ssp, work last 2 sts in 1 × 1 ribbing.

**Row 7:** Work 1 st of 1 × 1 ribbing, p2tog before marker, purl until next marker, ssp, work last 1 st in 1 × 1 ribbing.

### Increase Rows

**Row 1:** P in front and back loops of first st (pf&b), p1 before marker, purl until next marker, pf&b, end p1.

**Row 3:** Work 2 sts of 1 × 1 ribbing, pf&b before marker, purl until next marker, m1tbp, work 2 sts of 1 × 1 ribbing.

**Row 5:** Work 3 sts of 1 × 1 ribbing, pf&b before marker, purl until next marker, m1tbp, work 3 sts of 1 × 1 ribbing.

**Row 7:** Work 4 sts of 1 × 1 ribbing, pf&b before marker, purl until next marker, m1tbp, work 4 sts of 1 × 1 ribbing.

**Row 1:** Work 5 sts of 1 × 1 ribbing, pf&b before marker, purl until next marker, m1tbp, work 5 sts of 1 × 1 ribbing.

**Row 3:** Work 6 sts of 1 × 1 ribbing, pf&b before marker, purl until next marker, m1tbp, work 6 sts of 1 × 1 ribbing.

**Row 5:** Work 7 sts of 1 × 1 ribbing, pf&b before marker, purl until next marker, m1tbp, work 7 sts of 1 × 1 ribbing.

**Row 7:** Work 8 sts of 1 × 1 ribbing, pf&b before marker, purl until next marker, m1tbp, work 8 sts of 1 × 1 ribbing.

There are now 10 sts of ribbing on each edge again.

Continue to work even in patts as established for approximately 7½ (8½, 10)" (19 [21.6, 25.4]cm) from waistline, or to length desired between waist and underarm, ending after Row 8. In sizes as written, work measures 14¾ (17¼, 19⅔)" (37.5 [43.8, 49.9]cm) from beg and 6 (7, 8) additional reps of Spire patt have been worked.

## Shape Armholes

**Next Row (WS):** BO 8 (9, 9) sts in 1 × 1 ribbing. Work 2 (1,1) st(s) before marker as established. Work Spire patt Row 1 until marker. Work 1 × 1 ribbing to end of row.

**Next Row (RS):** BO 8 (9, 9) sts in 1 × 1 ribbing. Work 2 (1, 1) st(s) before marker in ribbing as established. Work Spire patt Row 2 until second marker. Work 2 (1, 1) st(s) after marker in ribbing as established.

Continuing to work in ribbing as established 2 (1, 1) st(s) before marker, and 2 (1, 1) st(s) after, work Spire patt, until piece measures approximately 6 (7½, 8½)" (15.2 [19, 21.6]cm) from beg of armhole shaping, ending after Row 8 after 5 (6, 7) additional reps of Spire patt.

## Shape Back Neck

Purl 58 (65, 73) sts. Put these sts on stitch holder #1. Purl across rem 18 (25, 33) sts (right shoulder).

**Row 2:** On active right shoulder sts, work st(s) before marker in ribbing as established, then work Row 2 of Spire patt to end of row.

**Row 3:** Purl 8 (8, 8) sts and put on stitch holder #2.

## Shape Right Shoulder

Work Rows 4–8 of Spire patt on rem 10 (17, 25) sts, working st(s) before marker in 1 × 1 ribbing as established.

BO pwise.

## Shape Left Shoulder

From stitch holder #1, pick up 18 (25, 33) sts at outer edge, leaving 40 (40, 40) sts on holder to form neckline.

Attach yarn at neck edge, beg with Row 2 of Spire patt, working st(s) after marker as 1 × 1 ribbing as established.

**Row 3:** Purl.

**Row 4:** Work 8 sts in Spire patt at neck edge. Put these 8 sts on stitch holder #3. Work in Spire patt until marker, working st(s) after marker as established.

Work rem sts in established patts for Rows 5–8.

BO pwise.

## Right Front

**note** The buttonhole will be placed relatively close to the collar. If you prefer to place your buttonhole at a different spot on your buttonband edging, follow the buttonhole instructions at your preferred location anywhere on the 1 × 1 ribbing.

CO 52 (60, 68) sts.

Set up patt as follows: Work edging of 1 × 1 Ribbing #1 for 10 sts. Pm. Work Row 1 of Spire patt until last 10 sts. PM. Work edging of 1 × 1 Ribbing #2 for 10 sts, slipping last st pwise to tighten up front edging. Continue to slip this last st at the front edge pwise each time you reach it at the end of a row. Work it regularly when it is at the beg of a row.

Continue working 10 sts of 1 × 1 Ribbing as established before marker, working 4 (5, 6) reps Spire patt between markers, and working 1 × 1 Ribbing as established after marker until work measures approximately 5 (6, 7½)" (12.7 [15.2, 19.1]cm) or until 2.5" (6.4cm) before reaching desired waistline. End after Row 8 of Spire patt; for average sizing, this will be after 4 (5, 6) reps of Rows 1–8.

## Waist Shaping

Follow instructions as for Back Waist Shaping

### Decrease Rows

**Row 1:** Work 8 sts of 1 × 1 ribbing, p2tog before marker, purl until next marker, work 1 × 1 ribbing.

**Row 3:** Work 7 sts of 1 × 1 ribbing, p2tog before marker, purl until next marker, work 1 × 1 ribbing.

**Row 5:** Work 6 sts of 1 × 1 ribbing, p2tog before marker, purl until next marker, work 1 × 1 ribbing.

**Row 7:** Work 5 sts of 1 × 1 ribbing, p2tog before marker, purl until next marker, work 1 × 1 ribbing.

**Row 1:** Work 4 sts of 1 × 1 ribbing, p2tog before marker, purl until next marker, work 1 × 1 ribbing.

**Row 3:** Work 3 sts of 1 × 1 ribbing, p2tog before marker, purl until next marker, work 1 × 1 ribbing.

**Row 5:** Work 2 sts of 1 × 1 ribbing, p2tog before marker, purl until next marker, work 1 × 1 ribbing.

**Row 7:** Work 1 st of 1 × 1 ribbing, p2tog before marker, purl until next marker, work 1 × 1 ribbing.

### Increase Rows

**Row 1:** P1 in front and back of first st (pf&b), p1 before marker, purl until next marker, work 1 × 1 ribbing.

**Row 3:** Work 2 sts of 1 × 1 ribbing, pf&b before marker, purl until next marker, work 1 × 1 ribbing.

**Row 5:** Work 3 sts of 1 × 1 ribbing, pf&b before marker, purl until next marker, work 1 × 1 ribbing.

**Row 7:** Work 4 sts of 1 × 1 ribbing, pf&b before marker, purl until next marker, work 1 × 1 ribbing.

**Row 1:** Work 5 sts of 1 × 1 ribbing, pf&b before marker, purl until next marker, work 1 × 1 ribbing.

**Row 3:** Work 6 sts of 1 × 1 ribbing, pf&b before marker, purl until next marker, work 1 × 1 ribbing.

**Row 5:** Work 7 sts of 1 × 1 ribbing, pf&b before marker, purl until next marker, work 1 × 1 ribbing.

**Row 7:** Work 8 sts of 1 × 1 ribbing, pf&b before marker, purl until next marker, work 1 × 1 ribbing.

When there are 10 sts of ribbing on each edge, continue to work even in patts as established for approximately 7½ (8½, 10)" (19 [21.6, 25.4]cm) from waistline, or to length between waist and underarm that matches back, ending after Row 8. In sizes as written, work measures 14¾ (17¼ ,19⅔)" (37.5 [43.8, 49.9]cm) from beg and 6 (7, 8) additional reps of Spire patt have been worked.

## Shape Right Armhole

**Next Row (WS):** BO 8 (9, 9) sts in 1 × 1 ribbing. Work 2 (1, 1) st before marker as established for ribbing. Work Spire patt Row 1 until marker. Work 1 × 1 ribbing to end of row.

Continuing to work patts as established, work 3 (3, 4) reps of Spire patt, until piece measures approximately 4 (4, 5)" (10 [10, 12.7] cm) from armhole, ending after Row 8.

### Work Buttonhole

**Row 1:** Work in patterns as established.

**Row 2:** Work 3 sts of ribbing. BO 5, work 2 sts of ribbing. Work Spire patt and 2 (1, 1) st(s) along armhole edge as established.

**Row 3:** Work patterns as established until second marker. Work 2 sts ribbing, CO 5 sts, work 3 sts ribbing.

**Row 4:** Work 10 sts 1 × 1 ribbing. Work Spire patt and st(s) along armhole edge as established.

Continue working patterns as established for Rows 5–8.

Work 0 (1, 1) rep of Rows 1–8 of Spire patt.

## Work Neckline Decreases

**Row 1:** Work in patterns as established.

**Row 2 (at neck edge):** BO 26 (26, 26) sts. Work patt until end of row.

**Row 3:** Purl as established.

**Row 4:** BO 8 (8, 8) sts. Work rem 10 (17, 25) sts as established in patt.

**Rows 5–8:** Work rem sts in patt until end of Row 8.

BO on purl row.

**note** Front armhole measurement as worked here will be approximately 1" (2.5cm) shorter than back armhole shaping. This allows the Spire patt to match up neatly.

## Left Front

Work as for Right Front instructions, until Waist Shaping.

## Waist Shaping

Work 4 reps of Rows 1–8 of Spire patt as follows. The process is the same as for the right front, with shaping taking place in the ribbing area during odd (WS) rows but on the opposite side of the piece. As before, the first 2 reps involve decreases while the second 2 reps involve increases.

### Decrease Rows

Work 2 reps (a total of 16 rows) with decreases at side edge on odd (WS) rows, as follows:

**Rows 1, 3, 5, and 7:** Work 42 (50, 58) sts as established (to second marker). After second marker, ssp, working rem sts in 1 × 1 ribbing to end of row.

### Increase Rows

Work 2 reps (a total of 16 rows) with increases at side edge on odd (WS) rows, as follows:

**Rows 1, 3, 5, and 7:** Work 42 (50, 58) sts as established (to second marker). After second marker, m1tbp in first st, work rem sts in 1 × 1 ribbing to end of row.

When there are 10 sts of ribbing on each edge, continue to work even in patterns as established for approximately 7½ (8½, 10)" (19 [21.6, 25.4]cm) from waistline, or to length between waist and underarm that matches back, ending after Row 8. In sizes as written, work measures 14¾ (17¼, 19⅔)" (37.5 [43.8, 49.9]cm) from beg and 6 (7, 8) additional reps of Spire patt have been worked.

## Shape Left Armhole

Work Row 1 as established.

**Next Row (RS):** BO 8 (9, 9) sts in 1 × 1 ribbing. Work 2 (1, 1) st(s) before marker as established for ribbing. Work Spire patt Row 2 until marker. Work 1 × 1 ribbing to end of row.

Continuing to work patterns as established, work 4 (5, 6) reps of Spire patt, or until length matches RF, ending after Row 8.

## Work Neckline Decreases

**Row 1** (at neck edge): BO 26 (26, 26) sts. Work patt until end of row.

**Row 2:** Work patt as established.

**Row 3:** BO 8 (8, 8) sts. Work rem 10 (17, 25) sts as established in patt.

**Rows 4–8:** Work rem sts in patt until end of Row 8.

BO off on purl row.

## Three-Quarter Length Sleeves (Make Two)

**note** Use a safety pin or marker to mark the RS. The fabric is largely reversible, but the cast-on edge will look more professionally finished on the RS.

CO 52 (60, 68) sts.

Working 1 × 1 ribbing #2 throughout sleeve, maintain patt, inc 1 st at beg and end of row every 5 (5, 5) rows 13 (15, 18) times for a total of 78 (90, 104) sts.

Continue in 1 × 1 ribbing until sleeve measures 12 (14, 16)" (30.5 [35.6, 40.6]cm) or desired length.

BO in 1 × 1 ribbing patt.

## Finishing

Align shoulders so Spire patt matches on fronts and back of sweater. With a tapestry needle and matching yarn, use the mattress st to join shoulders.

Align fronts and back at sides, matching up waist shaping, and, using a tapestry needle and matching yarn, sew side seams.

## Collar

**note** When picking up sts, calculate a rough measurement of 3 sts picked up for every 4 rows worked. The following approximate numbers are intended as a guide; add or subtract sts as necessary to create a collar without gaps or gathers.

**Row 1:** Pick up 40 sts across back of neck from stitch holder #1. With RS facing you, attach yarn at right-hand edge and work 1 row of 1 × 1 ribbing.

**Row 2:** Work 1 × 1 ribbing, continuing the row by putting 8 sts from stitch holder #2 on a needle and continuing to work 1 × 1 ribbing (48 sts).

**Row 3:** Work 1 × 1 ribbing. Pick up 8 sts from stitch holder #3 and cont ribbing. Cont this row by picking up an even number of sts, approximately 30 (36, 36) sts and working ribbing over shoulder and up to edge of, *but not across*, top of ribbed edging/button band.

**Row 4:** Work 1 × 1 ribbing with sts on a needle, continuing at the end of the row to pick up and work an even number of sts, approximately 30 (36, 36) sts, over shoulder and up to edge of, *but not across*, top of ribbed edging/button band.

Continue working 1 × 1 ribbing back and forth over all sts—approximately 116 (128, 128). When collar measures 4" (10cm) from buttonband edge, and center back measures 5" (12.7cm) or desired depth, BO in ribbing.

## Put in Sleeves

With sweater laid flat, mark top of each shoulder as "halfway" point for sewing in sleeves. This will be approximately 1" (2.5cm) above the shoulder seam. Folding each sleeve in half, align this point with the top of shoulder. Beg at the underarm, sew in sleeve with a tapestry needle and matching yarn.

Weave in ends.

Wash (according to ball band instructions) or dampen and dry flat to block, pinning out ribbing to stretch if necessary. Fold down collar and lapel above buttonhole as desired. Bear in mind that ribbing can be stretched through blocking, so if you'd prefer your sleeves to fit loosely, block the sleeves "hard" to create a less clingy garment.

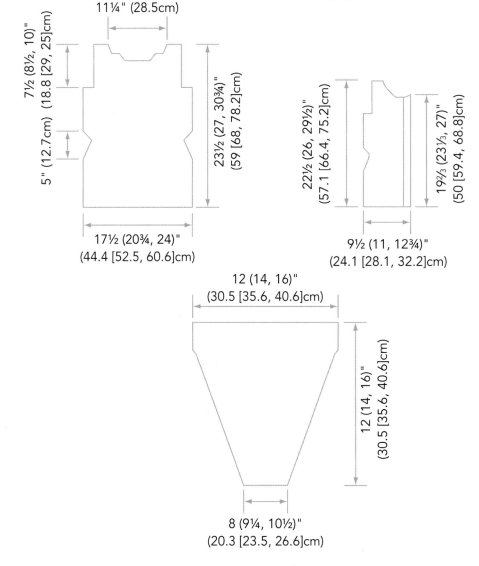

**Sew on Button**

Align the buttonhole with the opposite buttonband edging. Using matching thread and a sewing needle, attach button to smock. Use a smaller button on the WS of the smock as an anchor, and sew directly through the knitted material back and forth between the two buttons. This anchor button will help distribute the weight of a large button on the knitted materials so that the weight will be distributed evenly and will not damage your new sweater.

## ᔤ *Where Did You Get That Button?* ᔤ

A great way to find attractive, one-of-a-kind buttons for your sweaters is to cut them off old garments before reusing the material. Some people buy garments at secondhand stores just for their buttons. Or, you may be lucky enough to discover someone else's button collection at a yard sale or thrift shop. These special buttons allow for all kinds of creative choices; you may choose coordinating or even clashing buttons if you can't find six or eight that match on that next cardigan project. It's a good idea to go through your button stash every so often; not all button materials last forever. Leather buttons, in particular, may begin to crack or rot in changing weather conditions.

I'm lucky; both my mother-in-law and her mother had impressive button collections, which I have inherited. I continue to build on the collection by occasionally buying beautiful buttons, particularly ones made from natural or long-lasting materials like wood, pewter, or bone. I consider it an investment in the future. Someday, I hope to pass the collection along to a much younger knitter or seamstress!

If you've got just the right button, you may still be struggling over matching thread. While some may have a rainbow of sewing thread available locally, perfectly matching thread isn't always available for everyone, particularly if you don't have a fabric store nearby. Another option is to consider using embroidery floss in the right hue (use one or two strands at a time). A third choice is to find a color that matches or blends with your button, if not the colors of your sweater. This is also another opportunity to reuse or recycle. Ask a friend who embroiders if she might share her leftover threads at the end of a project. This "stash" of floss may well contain the right shade for your next set of sweater buttons, and you won't need a whole spool of thread to sew those on!

Reduce, Reuse,
Recycle

In 1991, when I was a freshman in college, I was handed a green plastic coffee mug. It read "Reduce, Reuse, Recycle." By now, practically everyone has heard of this phrase, and it's a great one to apply to fiber arts. This (now overly familiar) phrase is a handy way to talk about an important aspect of environmental conservation that we can easily incorporate into our knitting habits.

## Reduce

It's fashionable right now to buy our way toward sustainability. By that, I mean that we're tempted by flashy advertising of new, ever more environmentally friendly products… and I can't lie, these things tempt me as well! However, there are easy ways to reduce our consumption when it comes to knitting and make a small difference in reducing waste.

One reduction option is to actually knit from our stashes. Many knitters and spinners have such deep reserves of yarn saved up for special projects that we forget what we've got in the closet. Recently, I visited my family, and my mom, a long time knitter, and I went through her stash. We found yarn that I'd bought her as a present in 1992—right after I'd finished that freshman year of college! Sometimes it's worthwhile to use what we've got. It cleans out our closets and makes room for all the tempting things we do want!

Another way to reduce consumption is to trade with friends or give away yarns you're no longer interested in using. Often, those last three balls of hot pink angora lose their charm after you've knit an entire sweater out of it. Friends often have other treats that tempt you. Check out the information

included in this chapter on throwing a stash party, or do a trade with just one friend who shares your general style and taste. I've even done this entirely via e-mail and the post office—the exchange is just as satisfactory, although if you do it locally, the transport costs will be lower! You'll be overjoyed with your finds and the net result won't increase your stash, purchasing, or consumption.

Giving away yarns you feel you'll no longer use is also very freeing. Consider donating those yarns to a charity knitting group, a nursing home or assisted living center, or a group that teaches people how to knit. Even some prisons and homeless shelters have knitting programs and your leftover odds and ends can make a huge difference in someone's life.

## Reuse

Whenever one considers the ever increasing size of the local landfill, the notion of reuse becomes more important. There are so many ways that we can avoid discarding things by finding a new way to use them. Our society is called a "throw-away" one, and it doesn't have to be! While wealthy countries often enjoy the ability to purchase everything new, in truth, we can learn from poor communities,

*Yarn reclaimed from thrift store sweaters, ready to be knit into something new.*

who figure out how to reuse everything. When it comes to knitting, reuse is actually easy. Here are some simple suggestions.

## Frog It

We've all got unfinished knitting projects hiding in corners, waiting to be picked up again. The yarn was beautiful but the pattern wouldn't work out. The garment was the wrong size, or something more exciting popped up to be knit first. It can be remarkably freeing to reclaim yarn from an old project. Rip it out! (Frog it comes from the phrase, rip it! rip it!) Remember that visit to my mother's stash? She still has some luxury French yarn in a gorgeous rose color that she bought for me when I was a teenager. I got halfway through a sweater and the fashion changed; I lost interest. The yarn is now ready for her to knit something new. It's been waiting all this time!

Roll that yarn you've found into balls as you unwind your knitting. If the yarn is crinkly and needs to be flattened out, that's no problem. Make it into a skein (use a swift, a niddy-noddy, or even two chairs) and then gently

▼ *Reuse strips of fabric to create a brand-new garment.*

hand wash the skein without agitation. Hang it to dry, using a hanger as a weight if it still needs to be straightened out. Then start over with your "new" yarn!

If you're a newer knitter and lack a deep stash, you can still make use of this ripping technique. Go to thrift stores and look for high quality hand-knit sweaters. Read the labels and go for that luxury cashmere or Merino wool! This too can be reused and reknit. Remember to look for beautiful buttons too—sometimes it's worth the purchase of a worn out garment to cut off its buttons for something new. If you're nervous about how to choose sweaters that can be easily reclaimed as knitting yarn, try some Web searches for "recycled yarn" and you'll find some very useful tutorials online that take you through the process step by step. Even whole sweaters can be ripped out and reknit if you find you'd rather make something new. Just give yourself the chance to "unknit" and you'll be amazed with what you can produce the second time round.

▲ *Locally farmed, handspun yarn, dyed using recycled tea bags by Tara Swiger, the indie fiber artist behind Blonde Chicken Boutique.*

## While You're at the Thrift Store

Don't forget to look for yarn, needles, and patterns. Many knitters occasionally clean out their closets and donate unused items. Their loss can be your gain! Most of my straight needles come from yard sales and charity and thrift stores. I've amassed a huge collection of needles, from the smallest lace weight double points to hand-carved needles the size of broom sticks. You never know what will come in handy in your knitting career, so it's worthwhile to buy these finds when you come across them. Better yet, when I take some of these bone, wood, or metal needles in hand, I feel as though I am holding hands with women from past generations who loved to knit or crochet as much as I do.

Remember to isolate yarns found at thrift shops if they appear at all dirty or moth eaten. Skein and wash them thoroughly, if necessary, and take care not to bring home any pests like moths while you're shopping.

## Cones and Industry Discards

If you live near factories or other textile industries, you may be aware of industry seconds. This can be a wonderful bounty for a knitter, crocheter, spinner, or weaver. Many times, factories that manufacture yarn create odds and ends that they cannot sell or use. Perhaps they dyed a fiber the wrong color or the weaving machines can't use the last few

## ৪৩ *Stash Party* ৪৩

Everyone loves a party, and a stash swap is a fabulous way to get your friends together. The best swaps work when "the rules" are established in advance. Here are some pointers to make your party a success:

- ৪৩ Plan an event where the swap is only one part of the fun. Invite people to bring their knitting, spinning, quilting or other handiwork, have food and drink available, and create an environment where everyone has plenty of time to knit, chat, and feel at home. This way, if someone doesn't find a wonderful treat at the swap, he or she will still have a fun time.

- ৪৩ Make the swap's guidelines clear and explain them in advance. Should everyone at the party bring something to swap? Are all fiber arts materials fair game, or is this a knitting or crochet only swap? Is only yarn being exchanged, or tools, patterns, and other supplies as well? Are you attaching a monetary value to things being swapped? Does that matter for your crowd?

- ৪৩ Many guilds do swaps with fun games that allow some chance and luck to play a part. The items to be swapped are on a big table. Sometimes they are wrapped up so you can't see what you'll get. Some groups assign people numbers so that number one is allowed to go to the table first, but later numbers can

yards of yarn on each cone. This is essentially new yarn or roving that can't be utilized for its intended commercial project. Some of this is sold at factory shops as "mill ends" or donated to a nearby nonprofit or charity shop.

Usually the yarn or thread comes on cones rather than in skeins. It might need to be doubled or tripled, or the colors may need to be used creatively if there isn't enough of any one color on its own. However, choosing to knit with this yarn means you'll likely be saving a lot of money, getting a good

quality product, and keeping yarn from going to waste. If you think outside the box, you'll save money and produce gorgeous knitwear from these yarns.

"Cone yarns" are also a great way to reduce energy consumption. Sometimes when purchasing yarn, you have the choice between buying it on a cone or in a skein or ball. Cone yarns are likely to have fewer breaks, so you have fewer joins to contend with as you knit. Yarn producers must skein or wind each ball individually, and most use machines to do this task. As a result, purchasing your yarn

collect two treats rather than one. You may find complicated negotiations taking place between participants as well. It's important to emphasize that this is all in good fun! For fairness's sake, everyone should end up with something roughly equivalent to what she or he brought to the event. The exception might be a moving party, in which the person who is moving gives a lot of his or her stash away to friends as part of the farewell.

&. If planning a swapping event, take pains to explain your plans before people attend so no one brings something inappropriately valuable. One spinning guild swap I always enjoyed attending stipulated that you should donate something that you never wanted to see again! This meant that the swap table was filled with funny odds and ends—half of a 12-pound fleece because someone got tired of it, or bright orange boucle yarn that just never found the right project. Remember, "One man's trash is another man's treasure..." (Or is that "One woman's odd dye lot is another woman's pleasure?!")

&. The treasures I received from farewell parties, and gift or stash swaps were things I might never have bought, but thoroughly enjoyed in the end. If you don't live near others for a stash party, consider doing your swap online...and the postal service can be part of the fun—who doesn't love a package in the mail?

on a cone may be less expensive for you and for the company. In fact, just choosing cone yarns, even if they are brand new, saves a lot of money, as skeining and labeling yarn requires a lot of excess time and energy at the factory.

## What Fibers Should I Choose to Reuse?

When you are reusing previously knit yarns or industry mill ends, remember that whether or not any of this fiber was produced in an environmentally friendly way, it's here now so it's too late to worry over its origin. We need to use and reuse it in energy efficient ways. If you'd normally have qualms about using some fibers, this may be a special opportunity. Perhaps it's your chance to knit a hardwearing acrylic item without guilt—because when you pay for this at the thrift store, you're not funding the industry that created that petroleum-based acrylic in the first place. Or, perhaps you could never afford Italian crepe Merino or cashmere at market prices? Again, here it is—make use of what's available.

If you usually only buy locally produced knitting materials, consider that this fiber was purchased, trucked to a local store or factory, and processed near you. If you don't buy it and use it locally, it may well be shipped out again, thus increasing its carbon footprint through further transportation costs.

Reusing available resources locally is generally a good idea regardless of the product's origin. If a discarded garment or yarn is knit into something new without travelling thousands of miles, it keeps things out of landfills where you live. Also, many discarded textiles end up being shipped internationally for reuse and recycling, and it's best to avoid that additional travel and fuel expense if we can.

## Recycle

When you're finished with the cone of yarn, remember to recycle the cone itself—that cardboard is usually recyclable! Several projects in this book reuse materials, essentially recycling an item that's no longer of use into something we can use. Reuse an old sheet and make soft baskets for your home, or use stash yarns to create curtains.

There's even a project here that has the potential to reduce a lot of waste through reuse. If you knit yourself washable napkins, you'll be able to cut down on your use and disposal of paper napkins. Choosing to use knitted or cloth napkins is a great step toward reducing and reusing, but what if you can't give up those paper products? Consider buying recycled products only. That's a good use of fiber!

Knitted Curtain

# Knitted Curtain

Curtains are a household necessity that many people make for themselves, but many of the knitted curtains on the market are somewhat complicated and lacy. I'm not much of a lacy type in my home décor, but I do see the beauty in surrounding myself in knitting. Here's a simple way to use up some stash and knit yourself a light and airy modern looking curtain that offers some privacy but also brings in lots of light. The pattern is easy to adjust if you desire longer or wider curtain panels. If you wish for even more privacy, line the back of these curtains with a sheer or a muslin liner to allow light in. If you live in a colder climate and need protection from cold winds, invest in a thick insulating curtain as the first layer and hang your knitted curtain on top. Energy efficiency doesn't mean we have to give up beauty!

The curtain featured here is one of a kind, but I've provided generic yarn requirements so you can substitute yarns from your stash or those purchased to support your environmental goals. The yarn is handspun, created by Jan Geyer, a friend of mine. She chose to trade it with me at a swap party, and I've always loved the rich green tweedy color. However, you'll note the button tabs are not matching; one of a kind handspun, long marinated in my stash, didn't provide quite the yardage I needed. Instead of giving up on the project, I found coordinating colors and buttons and got busy. Many of us have interior design schemes with coordinating colors and themes; add your curtain design into the mix if you choose to use stash.

## Skill Level
Easy

## Size
One size (See pattern instructions for adjustments if necessary.)

## Finished Measurements
Blocked: 36" (91.5cm) wide × 52" (132cm) long

With standard curtain rod: 36" (91.5cm) wide × 50" (127cm) long

With button tabs: 36" (91.5cm) wide × 54" (137cm) long

## Materials
**note** Sample is made out of one-of-a-kind handspun from my stash. Please use the below information to choose yarn that meets your needs:

- 550 yd. (503m) of sport-weight wool yarn per panel, 7⅓ oz. (207g), 1,200 yd. per lb (2,413m per kilo) that knits at 5 sts to 1" (2.54cm) on U.S. size 3 (3.25mm) needles if you're knitting the buttoned tabs.

or

- 450 yd. (411.5m) of sportweight wool yarn per panel, 7⅓ oz. (207g), 1,200 yd. per lb (2,413m per kilo) if you are creating a café curtain for a regular curtain rod.
- U.S. size 15 (10mm) circular needle, 32" (80cm) or longer
- Row counter
- 7 buttons or beads, ⅜" (1cm) (optional, if knitting the buttoned tabs)
- Tapestry needle
- U.S. size 3 (3.25mm) double-pointed needles (optional, for buttoned tabs)
- Crochet hook (optional, for creating button loops)
- Sewing needle (optional)
- Matching thread (optional)

## Gauge

8 sts and 12 rows = 4" (10cm) in garter stitch with #15 (10mm) needles

20 sts and 22 rows = 4" (10cm) in stockinette stitch with #3 (3.25mm) needles

## Instructions

**note** Adjusting Curtain Length:

Curtain will be hung so it has vertical stripes. The CO sts will determine the length of the curtain. CO fewer sts for a shorter length curtain, or more sts for a longer length. Length can also be extended by creating longer buttoned tabs. Simply knit longer I-cord tabs (2" (5cm) for each 1" (2.5cm) of length desired) to add length.

**note** Adjusting Curtain Width:

Wider curtains can be created by several techniques. One option is to knit two panels for each window, thus creating 72" (183cm) of curtain width. Another option is to knit a wider panel, simply by repeating the garter st and stockinette pattern.

### Curtain

With #15 (10mm) needles, CO 100 sts.

Work 20 rows garter st. (Knit every row.)

Work 10 rows St st. (Knit 1 row, purl 1 row.)

Rep the above 30 rows until piece measures 36" (91.5cm) or desired width, ending with 20 rows of garter st. BO.

### Finishing

Weave in ends.

Block to measurements. Block according to yarn manufacturer's instructions, or as appropriate for the fibers used. Lay flat to dry.

**To hang Café style curtain:**

Fold over 2" (5cm) on one short side of curtain on WS to create a 2" (5cm) channel for a curtain rod. With a tapestry needle and matching yarn, whip st down this end on the WS of the curtain.

**To create tabs that can hang from a decorative pole or 1" rod:**

Create channel, as above, to reinforce top of curtain.

**Make seven I-cords for 36" (91.5cm) panel:**

With #3 (3.25mm) dpns and matching or coordinating colors of yarn, CO 5 sts.

Work I-cord for 7½" (19cm) or until desired length.

To BO, k2tog, k2tog, BO 1 st. K2tog, BO second st. Leave 1 st rem on needle.

With rem st, knit 8 rows or 1¼" (3.2cm) in length, or desired length to create button loop. This technique will resemble a single crochet chain, and if preferred, work this with a crochet hook and chain 8, or desired length to create button loop. BO.

Stitch buttons or large beads on each I-cord at the CO end of the button tab. Using a tapestry needle, join the end of the button loop to the beg to create a buttonhole. Evenly distribute the I-cord button tabs across the curtain: Insert the I-cord button tabs into the top of the curtain by poking one end of each I-cord loop through both layers of knitting to create loops to hang the curtain. Work across the curtain, taking care to align the buttons as desired. Hang on a decorative curtain rod through the button tabs.

Blocked Measurements

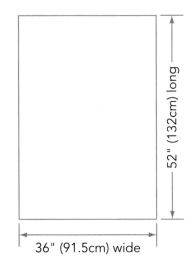

52" (132cm) long

36" (91.5cm) wide

# Waves and Stars: Knitted Napkins

Dress up your table with casual, bright knitted napkins! Using reusable linens is good for the environment; it vastly reduces the number of paper napkins we use. Regular paper napkins require the cutting down of trees to make the paper, and even recycled paper napkins rely on a lot of energy to produce, package, and ship the napkins to your local store. Consider switching to knitted and cloth napkins and help your table setting go upscale, too. This pattern includes two different square napkin designs. Each is knit with a machine washable and dryable worsted weight cotton blend yarn on #8 (5mm) needles. The Waves napkin uses two colors and is approximately 9" (23cm) square. The Stars pattern creates a reversible 8" (20cm) napkin in two colors with a fun texture.

## Skill Level
Easy

## Size
One size

## Finished Measurements
Waves: 9" (23cm) square
Stars: 8" (20cm) square

## Materials
- 3 skeins each of Knit Picks Shine Worsted yarn, 60 percent Pima Cotton, 40 percent Modal natural beech wood fiber, 75 yd. (68.5m), 1¾ oz. (50g) in the following colors:

**For Waves:**
- Color A: 23806 Reef
- Color B: 24142 Sailor

**For Stars:**
- Color A: 24144 Crème Brulee
- Color B: 23810 Terra Cotta

or

- For each set of napkins, 225 yd. (206m) each of two colors of machine washable worsted weight yarn that knits up at 4¼ sts to 1" (2.5cm). For both sets, 225 yd. (206m) each of four colors of yarn.
- U.S. size 8 (5mm) straight or circular needle, *or size to obtain gauge*
- Row counter
- Tapestry needle

## Gauge
17 sts and 24 rows = 4" (10cm) in stockinette stitch

## Pattern Stitches

### Waves Stitch Pattern

Row 1 is a WS row.

**Rows 1–5:** With Color A, knit.

**Rows 6 and 8:** With Color B, *k2tog, k2, kf&b in next 2 sts, k3, ssk; rep from *.

**Rows 7 and 9:** With Color B, purl.

**Row 10:** With Color A, *k2tog, k2, kf&b in next 2 sts, k3, ssk; rep from *.

**Rows 11–15:** With Color A, knit.

**Rows 16, 18, and 20:** With Color B, *k2tog, k2, kf&b in next 2 sts, k3, ssk; rep from *.

**Rows 17, 19, and 21:** With Color B, purl.

**Row 22:** With Color A, *k2tog, k2, kf&b in next 2 sts, k3, ssk; rep from *.

### Starry Stitch Pattern

**M1p (Make 1 purl st):** insert needle from behind under running thread between the stitch just worked and the next stitch, and purl this thread.

**Row 1:** (RS) With Color A, k1, *k3, pass first of 3 knit sts over the other 2 sts; rep from *, end k1.

**Row 2:** With Color B, p1, *M1p; p2; rep from *, end p1.

**Row 3:** With Color B, k2, *k3, pass first of 3 knit sts over the other 2 sts; rep from *.

**Row 4:** With Color A, p2, *M1p; p2; rep from *.

## Instructions

**note** Napkin sizes are flexible. These patterns may be worked in other gauges, in any machine washable yarn you wish to substitute, but the finished product may not come out the same size as the sample yarns featured here.

**note** When working with two colors, carry the second color along the edge of the napkin, twisting with the other color at the start of each edge row. This will avoid unnecessary ends that might poke out later.

**note** At the last st of each row where you knit or purl all the way across (without other st manipulations), with yarn in front, sl1 pwise to create a neat edge.

### Waves Napkin (Make Four)

With A (Reef), CO 44 sts on #8 (5mm) needles, *or size to give gauge.*

Work Waves Stitch patt 2 times.

Work Waves Stitch patt Rows 1–15.

BO with A.

**note** If you are making a napkin in a different size *or* have a different row gauge, rep Waves Stitch patt until the napkin is about 15 rows short of the desired length. Finish by working rows 1–15 and BO.

### Stars Napkin (Make Four)

With Color A (Crème Brulee), CO 47 sts.

Purl 1 row (WS row).

Work Starry Stitch patt, above. When napkin measures 8" (20cm), end with Row 4.

With A, BO.

### Finishing

Using a tapestry needle, weave in ends.

Block lightly.

Bon appétit!

Buy Local Goods

The idea of buying local products may seem familiar to you because we often hear it related to food purchases. However, it's relevant to our yarn, pattern, and book purchases, too...and in particular, to our natural fiber yarns. That's because natural fiber yarns are farm products. Like many foods, they are processed before ending up as yarns—and all these parallels make for some amazing metaphors. You'll find this chapter uses these parallels to draw conclusions. Why not focus exclusively on the statistics surrounding buying yarns locally? Well, as you might imagine, our economy makes many useful calculations around food growth, processing, and consumption. Despite the enormous value of yarn to knitters, there just aren't as many statistics around the costs of processing and shipping yarn large distances!

ॐ

In some areas, it's entirely possible to get amazing yarns that are grown and raised locally. If, for instance, you live in an area known for its traditional fiber producing and processing, like New England, there are lots of local options. This is also true for many other areas of the United States. In particular, small fiber mills scattered around the country may be able to provide gorgeous natural yarns, produced from locally grown fiber. You might even be able to buy patterns from local independent designers and books published by local authors. However, not every climate is conducive to every kind of fiber production, and some people cast the net of "local" more widely. If you see the United States or your entire country as "local," you can absolutely buy natural fiber yarns that are produced in one's own country.

Bear in mind, of course, that ideally, buying local doesn't merely mean that we drive only a few miles or kilometers to a local branch

of a large corporate store and buy the yarn there! In some cases, buying locally is easy, but in others, it requires quite an effort. Either way, your choice to buy local yarns (as well as foods) can only make a positive difference in a variety of ways. The concerns that cause people to buy local foods are nearly identical to the reasons why we might consider buying local fibers and yarns. Here are some of the arguments for buying local.

## Energy Consumption and Your Carbon Footprint

Imagine getting in the car, driving 750 miles (1,207km) across North America and stopping at a farm stand. At the farm stand, you can purchase not only vegetables and fruit, but also a leg of lamb and some skeins of yarn. Then, after that long weary day of driving, you

*Connecting with your local knitting community can offer opportunities to buy locally from small producers, like this small heritage breed-focused farm in Tennessee.*

▲ *Local spinners and dyers often sell their products through the local yarn store.*
*Shop owners are a great source of information about locally produced goods.*

put your purchases right into the car. You don't stop, because after all, you'd like to bring your purchases home, and you turn around and head in that direction. It takes you two long days of driving before you're ready to eat, and probably a few more days before you've recovered enough energy to start knitting!

Sound ridiculous? Of course it does—but many reliable sources say that, these days, our food purchased at the grocery store in the United States is likely to have travelled 1,500 miles (2,414km). There are local exceptions to this rule, but that just compensates for the Australian or New Zealand leg of lamb that travelled ever so much farther to be on your table.

If you're wondering what this has to do with yarn…remember, wool comes from sheep… that same flock that possibly offered up that leg of lamb for your dinner table! Cotton and linen come from fields of cotton or flax plants…and so on. Right now, agricultural products are shipped thousands of miles or kilometers across the globe. Every shipment uses energy, likely natural gas, coal, and oil, to arrive at its destination. These energy sources aren't renewable resources, and according to many accounts, unless we start conserving these resources, they will run out. We're depending on those nonrenewable energies not only to drive to the yarn shop, but also because trucks, fueled by gas, deliver the yarn to the yarn shop. The yarn has to be processed from the natural, raw fiber—and that usually consumes nonrenewable energy, too.

Furthermore, the burning of these fossil fuels produces a lot of greenhouse gases, such as carbon dioxide. Those gases lead to seriously negative effects on our environment, such as global warming. The term carbon footprint comes from what our activities cause—that is, the amount of carbon dioxide (and other greenhouse gases) we're leaving behind in the environment.

Those yarns being shipped are packaged into bags, boxes, or crates to be transported. Before it was yarn, the raw fiber was transported in bales or bags to the mill to be processed. At each stage, there was packaging that kept your future knitting or crochet project clean and undamaged. It takes a lot of energy to produce packaging materials, just as it takes energy to produce the items inside. The packaging itself may weigh a lot (costing more to be shipped), be produced from nonrenewable resources, or be made in a way that it can't be recycled. The end result is that some yarns have an enormous carbon footprint. While knitting at home doesn't seem like it could harm the environment, those yarns just might.

For instance, imagine a sheep station in Australia grows gorgeous Merino. That raw Merino is shipped perhaps 10,000 miles (16,000km) to Italy to be washed and processed into yarn. It's then labeled and packaged and shipped to distribution centers in each country it will be sold in, such as the United States and Canada. It's shipped possibly thousands of miles or kilometers from the distribution center on one coast to your local

yarn shop on the other coast. You drive to the yarn shop, purchase your yarn, and bring it home. Once all that transport is considered, I'm sure you'll feel that skein of yarn was remarkably inexpensive, but the expense is in all those gallons or liters of gas and oil that were used to get it to your home. While your local options for purchase might be slightly more limiting, when considering the transport costs, suddenly, paying for locally grown and processed wool yarn whenever possible might seem downright affordable.

What about patterns and books? Consider that many books are printed less expensively in Asia, but the shipping and production environmental cost and pollution can be large. A locally printed book (on recycled paper!) is less detrimental to the environment. Single patterns, published locally by independent designers, end up being less expensive to purchase or ship, and the best option of all for "local" pattern consumption might be downloading patterns off the Internet. Yes, you use electricity, but there are no transport costs, and pollution costs are very low when you download from home!

# Agriculture and Family Farms

For many centuries, most of our food and textiles came from small farms owned by families. These small farms produced food and fiber beyond their own needs, and the farm families made a living by selling this bounty in the closest town market. In these small "ecosystems," farmers might trade raw wool for handspun yarns, produced by women who lived in the nearby town. Spinners in a family might pool their yarns and bring it to a talented weaver, who wove that yarn into cloth for both their families and the farm family. Through small town cooperation and commerce, textiles were processed and worn within just a few miles of where they were grown.

With the growth of industrialized farming, this pattern has changed. According to United States Department of Agriculture statistics, the United States has lost 5 million farms since 1935. While large industrial farms are celebrated as "efficient" and "cost saving," they can do harm to the environment because of the large scale monoculture farming taking place. As mentioned in chapter 1, maintaining small ecosystems is important to the world's environmental health. Local and small farmers tend to have a stake in their land. Small farmers live on their land and often want to preserve it for future generations. It's also likely they'll want to avoid environmental pollutants that might harm their crops, livestock, and families. This small landowner's efforts toward environmental protection can be lost with the loss of family farms.

According to www.sustainabletable.org, a Web site that offers information about local sustainable food, "By supporting local farms near suburban areas and around cities, you help keep farmers on the land, and, at the same time, preserve open spaces and counteract urban sprawl." If we take that a step further, we can see that by choosing to live in areas that help protect farmland, we not only preserve the environment and rural communities, but we also protect a local supply of food and textiles. If our town's zoning prevents sprawl and allows small farms to keep

sheep or grow cotton, we'll have much better access to locally grown and natural fibers. That locally grown product is a wonderful asset to a community's resources in an era of reduced fossil fuel availability and hence, increased shipping expense or lack of supplies from elsewhere.

## Supporting Your Local Economy

At first, this aspect of buying local is hidden. When you purchase locally made items, more of your money stays in the local economy. So, in the best sense, one would hope to buy a yarn very locally, where the sheep or alpacas grazed nearby, the fiber mill was in your community, and you could purchase those wool/alpaca blend yarns directly from the farm. In this example, any money that didn't go directly to the farmer would go to that local business, the fiber mill. However, even if, say, you're buying hand-dyed yarns where only the dyeing takes place locally, you'll still be making a difference in that local hand-dyer's bottom line.

Putting your money back into the local economy may be very meaningful. Again, the metaphor of the grocery store is useful here—because this information is widely available, unlike yarn statistics! Farmers that provide produce or other basic ingredients like wheat to commercial grocery store chains can only expect to earn perhaps 10 to 20 cents of each dollar you spend in the store. Most of the money goes to pay for suppliers, processors, distributors, and marketers. In short, the middlemen get most of the money you pay.

In contrast, purchasing from your local farmer at a farmer's market will likely earn that farmer 80¢ to 90¢ of each dollar you spend. (The farmer usually pays a fee for his stand at the market—that's where the rest of the dollar may go, along with transportation costs to market.) Those 80¢ to 90¢ allow the farmer to leave his stand for a moment and spend more money at other farmers' stands to support his own business. The farmer can invest in locally grown feed for his fiber animals or local homemade sheep's cheese for his family. His purchase of that feed or cheese puts money back into your community—as the cheese maker goes to buy something else local. The cheese maker also raises sheep that possibly eat local grain, and those sheep will need to be shorn…and that flock offers you a local supply of wool, and perhaps even the occasional lamb chops for your dinner table.

By purchasing local products, you keep your money circulating and boosting your local economy. Even better, there's a good chance that if the farmer can afford that other local product, the cheese maker or grain farmer can afford to continue to supply it. By choosing to put money into local purchases, you ensure a greater likelihood that more people will start local small businesses because they'll see a demand for their products.

This model sounds wonderful, but not everybody has access to local products direct from the farm. There are other ways to "buy local." One option is to seek out farmers' markets and other fiber sources that are slightly farther away—even if you must drive a distance, the value of those purchases will reverberate in your area's economy. If you'd rather order online and stay home, shipping yarn or a fleece from a farm business 100 miles (161km) away is far better than shipping from across the world.

If you have a favorite local yarn store, choosing to buy your yarns locally (even if they are produced across the world) can help maintain the presence of an independently owned knitting shop. It can also create community in your area even while it has to compete with big box stores or perhaps less expensive Internet yarn sales. You can choose to both support your local yarn shop and buy local if you encourage your shop owner to offer locally grown yarns for sale. A locally handspun or hand-dyed yarn, sold at a fair price, will provide a dyer or spinner with an income. If the yarn shop sells a locally designed pattern or published book, this supports a knitwear designer or writer and allows her a living in your community. Again, remember that these product choices may cost more than mass-produced yarns shipped halfway across the world, but your money will go toward paying that spinner or designer's grocery bills instead of toward global transportation costs.

If you absolutely must purchase that precious Australian Merino online, well, that temptation has happened to the best of us. Take care to order all you need at once. Purchase from a reputable shop that will invest money into its community—wherever it is in the world. Ship larger parcels of yarn or fiber, rather than buying one tidbit at a time because purchasing in bulk reduces the shipping, packaging, and transportation costs for each skein of yarn, knit lovingly, at home.

Gator Gaiter

# Gator Gaiter

This scarf has all the charm of a quick knit with a sophisticated look at the end. It's flexible in terms of yarn choice; choose something you can purchase locally, spin your own yarn, or raid your stash! Each end features a 5" (12.5cm) triangle point with a CO or BO of just 3 stitches, and an offset stitch, which widens out to a rectangular scarf in the middle. The shorter gator gaiter is knit with a locally hand-dyed, double strand of fingering weight yarn that knits up as a DK weight yarn. The longer gator gaiter is knit with one strand of a special DK weight handspun cashmere yarn from my stash.

Purchased from a United States citizen who bought it directly from the goat herder while living in Asia, this cashmere was sold to spinners to defray the costs of her trip. My portion of the cashmere was dehaired at a fiber mill in the United States, and I spun it during a terrible late night thunderstorm. While this fiber wasn't raised "locally" to me, it came straight from a goat farm and was sold directly to me from a friend of that Asian goat herder. You can read more about this exact skein of yarn in the book *KnitLit the Third: We Spin More Yarns*, edited by Linda Roghaar and Molly Wolf (Three Rivers Press, 2005) There are lots of options to create an individualized look with this scarf—double an indie dyed fingering weight sock yarn, or use a high-end DK weight luxury one. If you live in a cold climate, knit the longer scarf, which will allow you to wrap the scarf around the neck twice. Then, leave your scarf ends open or pin it closed with a special pin.

**Skill Level**
Easy

**Size**
Both shorter and longer gaiter fit all sizes

**Finished Measurements**
27 (52)" (68.6 [132]cm) long × 5½" (14cm) wide

**Materials**

**For shorter gaiter:**
- 1 skein of Enchanted Yarn and Fiber Bamboo Blend Sock Yarn, 60 percent Superwash Merino/30 percent Bamboo/10 percent Nylon, 440 yd. (402m), 4 oz. (113.4g), color Pixie Blush

or

- 150 yd. (137m) of any DK weight yarn with the appropriate gauge

or

- 300 yd. (274m) of any fingering weight yarn, doubled, with the appropriate gauge

**For longer gaiter:**

- 1 skein handspun cashmere 2 ply DK weight yarn, 100 percent cashmere, 230 yd. (210m), 3 oz. (85g), naturally white

or

- 240 yd. (219m) of any DK weight yarn with the appropriate gauge

or

- 480 yd. (439m) of any fingering weight yarn, doubled, with the appropriate gauge
- U.S. size 5 (3.75mm) straight needles or circular needle, *or size to obtain gauge*
- Tapestry needle

## Gauge

22 sts = 4" (10cm) in Blanket Rib stitch with DK weight yarn or fingering weight yarn knitted double. It's not necessary to calculate row gauge to knit this design, but if you're curious, row gauge is 24 rows = 4" (10cm) for the hand-dyed yarn and 26 rows = 4" (10cm) for the handspun cashmere.

## Pattern Stitch

### Blanket Rib Stitch

**Row 1 (WS):** Kf&b in each st.

**Row 2 (RS):** K2tog, *p2tog, k2tog, rep from * to end.

## Instructions

### Form Triangle

With fingering weight yarn doubled, or 1 strand of DK weight yarn, CO 3 sts.

Work Row 1 as in Blanket Rib st, above.

**Row 2:** K2, * p2tog, k2tog, rep from *, to end.

**Row 3:** Work as Row 1.

**Row 4:** K2, *p2tog, k2tog, rep from * to last 2 sts, p2tog.

Rep above Rows 1–4 until there are 21 sts on the needle. End after Row 4.

Work Blanket Rib st for 15 (40)" (38 [101.5]cm); end after Row 2.

### End Triangle

**Row 1 (WS):** Work as Blanket st Row 1.

**Row 2 (RS):** K3tog, p3tog, *k2tog, p2tog, rep from * to end.

**Row 3:** Work as Blanket st Row 1.

**Row 4:** K3tog, p3tog,*k2tog, p2tog, rep from * to last 2 sts. K2tog.

Rep above Rows 1–4 until there are 3 sts on the needle. The final row of patt will be k3tog, p3tog, k2tog. BO the final 3 sts.

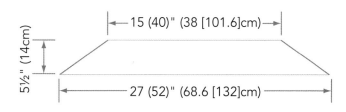

15 (40)" (38 [101.6]cm)

27 (52)" (68.6 [132]cm)

5½" (14cm)

Soft Basket

# Soft Basket

Ever notice that most of the baskets and containers available to contain kid or dog toys are made from polyester or plastic? Here's a way to create a soft sided basket ideal for clearing up clutter and collecting and containing all those little odds and ends. Plus, this basket is machine washable and you'll reuse an old bed sheet at the same time! If you don't happen to have an extra flat sheet around the house, purchase one in a color you like at a thrift shop, throw it in the wash, and get going on your basket. Once you've made one of these, you'll see how easy it is to adjust the pattern…larger baskets just require more stitch increases for the base, and smaller baskets use fewer stitches and rounds of knitting.

## Skill Level
Easy

## Size
One size

## Finished Measurements
12" (30.5cm) base × 7" (17.8cm) height with a 10" (25.4cm) opening

(Measurements are approximate; your basket may vary slightly.)

## Materials
- 1 full/double size flat bed sheet, which usually measures 78" × 100" (198cm × 254cm)—this is approximate, measurements vary—cut into 2" (5cm) wide strips of "yarn." (Instructions for creating strips follow.)

or

- Approximately 108 yd. (99m) of any weight of yarn that, knitted together, produce a super bulky yarn with the appropriate gauge
- Sewing scissors
- Ruler or tape measure
- U.S. size 19 (15mm) double-pointed needles, 12" (30cm) long, *or size to obtain gauge*
- U.S. size 19 (15mm) circular needle, 16" or 24" (40cm or 60cm) long, *or size to obtain gauge* (optional)
- Very large stitch markers, or rubber bands to use as stitch-marker substitutes
- Large crochet hook (optional)
- Elmer's glue (optional)
- 16 gauge electric fence wire (optional)
- Wire cutters (optional)

## Gauge
6 sts and 7 rows = 4" (10cm) over stockinette stitch

# Instructions

## Create Bed Sheet Yarn

First, remove the large hem at the top of the bed sheet by cutting or ripping it off. Then, measure 2" (5cm) from edge of sheet and make a small cut there. See Figure 1 for a visual version of this process. Using the cut as a guideline, tear the sheet until just about 2" (5cm) before the next corner. Use the scissors and ruler to measure 2" (5cm) from the edge of the sheet at the corner, make a small cut to guide you, and rip again. Continue on in this way until the whole bed sheet is one continuous strip.

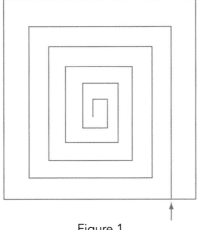

Figure 1

If you should tear a strip and forget to stop 2" (5cm) before the corner, it is no big deal. (We all make mistakes while ripping things!) Join the two strips as follows:

Cut a small buttonhole in the end of each strip:

Figure 2

Feed one strip through the buttonhole of the other strip. Put the other end of the strip you just put through the buttonhole, through the rem buttonhole, pulling until the join is snug. Your join should look like this:

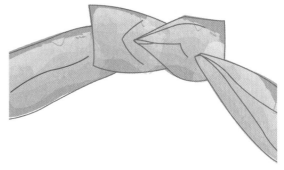

Figure 3

Wind the strip into one big ball of "yarn." Begin knitting by following the instructions below.

**note** Work increases by knitting in the front and back of the same stitch.

## Basket Base

CO 6 sts using the Figure Eight or Eastern Cast-On.

Knitting loosely, inc (kf&b) in each st, for a total of 12 sts. Distribute the sts evenly on 3 dpns. There will be 4 sts on each needle. Pm (use a rubber band as a convenient large-sized marker) and join.

**Rnds 1–4:** Work even, increasing 1 st at the end of each needle, until there are a total of 24 sts, 8 sts on each needle.

**Rnd 5:** *K3, inc 1 st in next st, pm, k3, inc 1 in next st, rep from * 2 more times.

Continue knitting in the round, always increasing 1 st before marker and 1 st at end of each needle.

When there are 16 sts on each dpn, or a total of 48 sts, stop increasing.

## Basket Sides

If your dpn set has five needles, redistribute the sts onto four needles at this point for convenience's sake, or beg using a circular needle.

Work even, taking care to knit loosely and not drop any sts off the ends of the dpns.

When 7" (17.8cm) of straight knitting is completed, basket reaches desired height or only 3–4 yd. (1m) of yarn strip remains, BO as follows:

*K2tog, k1, BO; k1, BO. Rep from * until all sts are BO. This creates a slightly smaller lip edge to your basket.

## Finishing

Weave in ends with your fingers, or with a large crochet hook. Trim any strip edges that poke out in an unattractive way. This creates a soft, entirely washable basket.

Should you want a stiffer basket, consider either of the following finishing techniques. Bear in mind that neither will maintain its shape if washed. Neither of the following will be safe for small children or animals.

## Glue

Using Elmer's glue, stripe the inside of the basket with the glue and spread with a finger or a piece of cardboard. Shape the basket as you'd like it to dry. When the glue is dry, it will create a slightly stiffer basket.

## Wire

Use electric fence wire to weave inside the basket to create stiffer structure. Create vertical staves with the wire, winding it into the purl side of the sts, or horizontal hoops. Use wire cutters to trim electric fence wire edges. Take care not to hurt yourself with the wire edges.

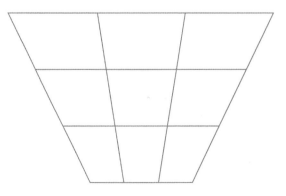

Figure 4

# Changing
# Our Habits

It's so hard to make even small adjustments to our daily routines. We're bombarded with commercialism in our society, and that pushes us in some difficult directions. We also may feel pressure from outside forces such as family, friends, or economic issues that make change hard. Often making the choice to spend less, recycle, or reuse materials may seem chintzy. That image can be daunting for some folks at the local knitting circle. What are ways to cope with both changing our habits toward living a more sustainable existence and helping others around us to consider or accept change?

Throughout this book, there have been multiple different ideas for how to make one's knitting choices carefully. Habits die hard—we make many choices every single day (and not just about knitting) because that's what we've always done! Making sustainable choices may require us to think more often about what it is we value. In a budget conscious time, we also have to decide where our money is best spent.

Exercising our brains by thinking is actually free. We can stop, imagine a different outcome, and then figure out how to save energy, time and other resources. In the knitting context, here's a scenario that might require thought and help you envision a different outcome. Let's say you love going to the local yarn store as a treat. (Who doesn't?)

We can support our local yarn stores by choosing yarns carefully based on the fibers, the production method, or because it benefits a women's co-op in Nepal. What are small steps toward change? There's that plan to spend judiciously and to consider where and to whom our funds go. Beyond that, consider taking public transportation, a walk, or a bike ride to the yarn

shop if that's possible. If your purchase is too unwieldy to make it home this way, should you buy anything in that quantity? Is it necessary?

If the yarn shop is too far away to enable a walk or bicycle ride, and public transport doesn't exist in your town, consider carpooling with a friend. Make a trip to the yarn shop a social encounter as well as a chance to purchase yarn. Enlist your friend so that the two of you can exert positive peer pressure on each other when it comes to your yarn purchases. Sometimes a friend can help you have a bit more restraint!

If your friend is also considering "going green" in some portion of his or her life, ask that friend to help you evaluate your own choices. We get used to how our homes look, our car trips, our clothes choices, and we forget to think about it. A kind friend not only helps change your light bulbs to more energy efficient ones, but also possibly helps you find that perfect knitting pattern for a new reusable shopping bag. Putting our heads together can result in some fascinating and positive life changes. It's also good to feel as though you aren't the only one thinking

*Consider bicycling to your local yarn store the next time you need to stock up.*

▶ *Vintage buttons, awaiting reuse.*

about this. It can help to know that "She's doing it, too!"

It can be difficult to break one's everyday routine—whether it's a resolution to cut down on doing excess driving or to purchase only local yarns. Some old habits are hard to break, even if they cost more, are less energy efficient, or are otherwise a bad idea. So, after we think about the change we'd like to make, how can we motivate ourselves to make it happen?

## Organize for Reduced Consumption

Let's say you've discovered that you have 8 identical U.S. size 6 (4mm) circular needles. (Oops.) This is because, like many of us, you forget the needles you've got at home when you're pondering a new project at the yarn shop. You also tend to have several projects going at once (sound familiar?) and therefore need several size 6 needles. However, you'd like to avoid purchasing another circular needle of the same size in the future, which is a logical way to cut down on waste.

Take some time to make a list of all your needles. Put that list in a knitting notebook, or make a copy of the list to carry in your purse. Having the list will help you realize what you do (and don't) need the next time you plan a big project.

If you're truly organized, you may want to consider using Ravelry or another kind of database to catalog your stash, knitting books, and patterns. In all honesty, I've managed to make my own knitting needle list in a knitting notebook, but not a database. I'm not quite ready to tell the world (or even myself) all of what's in my own yarn stash!

## Knit for Personal Change

Knitting can enable us to attempt even bigger energy efficiencies in a variety of ways. As an example, what about adjusting the thermostat? We can save a lot of energy and wear and tear on the environment simply by lowering the heat or using less air conditioning. Mr. Rogers *and* President Carter recommended wearing warm cardigans inside in the winter. We can do the same—with hand-knit socks besides!

Here are a few hints to make this adjustment viable in the winter if you're used to something much warmer. First, it's useful to have a thermostat that automatically adjusts your house's temperature so that it can be warmer during the day than at night. For instance, in my household in the winter time, the thermostat is set around 65 to 68 degrees F (18–20 degrees C) during the day. At night, the temperature can be set much lower, perhaps 55 to 63 degrees F (13–17 degrees C) because everyone is cuddled up in bed. When friends have bristled at what they see as overly cold temperatures, I loan them a sweater or two, hand-knit, of course.

In order to make this change, which saves a lot of energy and money, we have winter clothes that are far warmer than summer clothes. We don't wear short sleeves or miniskirts when it's cold around here. Wool hand-knit socks and sweaters are the uniform! At night, we have wool mattress pads, down comforters, and handmade wool afghans. Since I often kick off my covers, I tend to wear warm pajamas, including a sweater, to bed. I have a real motivation to provide my household with a steady stream of warm winter wear.

When springtime comes, you can bet we are ready to celebrate warmer weather by putting away the woolens, inching up the thermostat quite a bit, and sweating some. We're ready for the change...and I start knitting loose cotton tanks instead so we don't have to use the air conditioner too much!

# Birds of a Feather Flock Together

One of the most difficult transitions when choosing to make sustainable environmental decisions may be coping with the reactions of friends and family. Although these aren't knitting examples, they may be ones you've encountered...when my parents visit, my mother is astonished by the small amount of trash we produce. In trying to reduce our impact on the environment, we buy things with less packaging, we reuse and recycle materials, and compost some of our kitchen waste. As a result, when I last visited my parents, they showed me their improved recycling efforts with big smiles. I, of course, smiled right back! All recycling is good recycling when it comes to lowering the impact of our waste on local landfills.

We can positively influence our friends and families to make sustainable choices, whether it's about knitting, clothing and textiles, or in general. It's also great to find a knitting group or bunch of friends who usually support your choices. As individuals, it can be hard to

maintain green habits when surrounded by people who don't value our efforts. There are plenty of folks who care about environmental issues—and it might be worthwhile to make connections with others who value the same things as you do. While our extended families' households might not make big changes, we can always volunteer to knit that organic cotton baby blanket for a newborn, to make warm sweaters for when they visit your home, or just smile and approve of their recycling efforts.

# Innovation and Thinking Outside the Box

Thinking and learning creatively can help make a big difference when trying to conserve—no matter what you're trying to conserve. You may choose to cut back on expenses, on man-made fibers, on your carbon footprint—whatever your priorities, sometimes it helps to be creative. Knitters are known for being creative people, and that creativity can spill over to making big changes in your efforts toward sustainability. Here are some ways to make change by thinking outside the box.

- **Be Flexible:** Many knitters look at a magazine pattern and focus on the exact yarn requirements mentioned in the pattern, right down to the choice of color! If you can read the gauge in a pattern, you can substitute another kind of yarn that knits at the same gauge. Remember, too, that sometimes yarn colors are discontinued and those colors may go on sale...another way to save money on the project. If you'd rather focus on only natural-colored yarns that do not use dyes, again, substituting is often the best way to go. Give yourself the leeway to make your experience successful!

- **Plan to Cooperate:** If you've got other friends who share your values, consider buying yarn in bulk to save on the shipping and transportation costs. Plan a swap party to liven up or reduce your stash. Offer friends yarn or pattern trades (trading only original patterns and not copied ones—copied patterns violate copyright laws) to reinvigorate your knitting. Ask your friends to help convince a local yarn shop that there's a demand for offering locally produced yarns for sale. Don't feel you have to make all your changes alone.

- **Keep Learning:** Many knitters learn to spin or weave sooner or later. While the equipment involved in spinning and weaving can be expensive, it doesn't have to be. With a drop spindle or a simple loom, you can produce beautiful work. Spinners can purchase local wool and other fibers. Weavers can spin or purchase locally produced yarns. Both spinners and weavers really make things from scratch for their households—thus lessening their carbon footprint and creating exactly the yarns and woven goods they want. Even if you don't find spinning or weaving to be your thing, you can keep acquiring new knitting and crochet techniques that allow you to create innovative and new items for your efforts toward conservation.

- **Recycle and Reuse:** Learning to recycle your yarns from old sweaters and reusing others' leftovers can require a bit of courage and innovation in the beginning. Not everyone feels comfortable going through thrift stores for others' cast-offs, even if they are good quality wool or cashmere! If you feel queasy about this but want to do it, remember to wash everything carefully and thoroughly when you get it home. As soon as it has "your smell" you'll be much more brave about learning to unravel and reknit it!

- **Doubling Up:** If you reclaim yarn from thrift store sweaters, purchase cone yarns, or try to use up your stash, you may find that these yarns knit up at a different gauge than the patterns you'd like to knit. Sometimes you can knit double or triple strands of these yarns, or pair two colors and knit them together. It can take some experimentation to come up with a combination of yarns that knits at the right gauge for the project you have in mind. However, once you've hit on the "magic formula" of yarn weight, your knitting will speed along with the satisfaction of knowing you've innovated successfully to produce what you want!

In the end, no matter how much thinking we do, it takes personal change and innovation to break our habits and create new ones. Of all the green choices in this book, the ones that require changing habits may be the most difficult to establish. That doesn't mean change is impossible—just difficult! If you decide to make a big effort in regard to changing your habits, remember to take it one thing at a time. Within no time, you may have put a monthly visit to a neighborhood thrift store to search for beautiful cashmere sweaters (to reuse as yarn, of course) into your routine. Also, we all fall off the bandwagon every now and again. Be patient as you adjust to a "buy local only" resolution—especially if you need something "foreign" like silk as much as your fair trade coffee. Sometimes change happens slowly and in small steps. Every step, no matter how small, makes an important difference. Small steps toward sustainability accumulate toward a greener world—and a feeling that we're each doing our part.

**Cozy Zip-Up Cardigan**

# Cozy Zip-Up Cardigan

Just like Mr. Rogers or President Carter, we can always put on a sweater at home. Go ahead, lower the thermostat this winter! This unisex bulky weight Merino cardigan fits the (less expensive heating) bill perfectly; it's as soft as a cotton sweatshirt but as we knitters know, wool's warmer. Attractive saddle shoulder shaping and a low-key pattern contribute to a good fit and add flattering details. Best of all, with a zipper, one can fold over the edges for a V-neck collar effect, or zip right up to warm up your neck. This sweater is designed in multiple sizes so it can be knit to fit everyone in the family.

## Skill Level
Easy

## Size
XS (S, M, L, XL, XXL)

## Finished Measurements
Chest: 36 (41, 44, 50, 52, 57)" (91.4 [104.1, 111.8, 127, 132.1, 144.8]cm)

## Materials
- 7 (8, 9, 10, 11, 12) skeins of Morehouse Merino Bulky yarn, 100 percent Merino wool, 102 yd. (93m), approximately 4 oz. (113.4g), color Navy

or

- 714 (816, 918, 1,020, 1,122, 1,224) yd. (653 [746, 839, 933, 1,026, 1,119]m) of any bulky weight yarn with the appropriate gauge
- U.S. size 13 (9 mm) set of straights or circular needle, 24" (60cm) long, *or size to obtain gauge*
- 2 stitch markers
- Tapestry needle
- Matching separating zipper measuring 27 (27, 30, 30, 30, 32)" (68.6 [68.6, 76.2, 76.2, 76.2, 81.3]cm) in length, or length to zip-up cardigan as desired

**note** Sample zipper is from www.zipperstop.com, YKK #5 Molded Plastic Separating Zipper. Standard zipper lengths are 27", 30" and 36" (68.6 [76.2, and 91.4]cm). Custom lengths can be made for a small additional fee. Complete and block your garment and then measure the opening without stretching the fabric to determine zipper length.

- Sewing needle and matching thread
- Pins (optional)

## Gauge

10 sts and 16 rows = 4" (10cm) in Broken Rib patt

## Pattern Stitch

### Broken Rib worked over an even number of sts

**Row 1 (WS):** *K1, p1, rep from * to last st, wyif, sl1 pwise.

**Row 2 (RS):** Knit.

Rep Rows 1–2 for patt.

### Broken Rib worked over an odd number of sts

**Row 1 (WS):** *K1, p1, rep from * until last 2 sts, k1, then for last st, wyif, sl1 pwise.

**Row 2 (RS):** Knit.

Rep Rows 1–2 for patt.

# Instructions

## Back

CO 45 (51, 55, 61, 65, 71) sts.

Work in Broken Rib patt until the back measures 15 (15½, 15½, 16, 16, 16½)" (38.1 [39.4, 39.4, 40.6, 40.6, 41.9]cm). End with Row 2.

## Shape Armhole

Maintain Broken Rib patt as established throughout shaping of armholes and shoulders.

At the beginning of the next 2 rows, BO 3 (3, 3, 3, 4, 4) sts.

For all sizes, at the beg of following 2 rows, BO 2 sts.

Dec 1 st at beg and end of every RS row 1 (2, 2, 3, 3, 5) times; 33 (37, 41, 45, 47, 49) sts rem.

Continue working even until armholes measure 7½ (8½, 9, 9¼, 9¾, 10)" (19 [21.5, 23, 23.5, 25, 25.5]cm). End after Row 2 of patt.

## Shape Shoulders

At beg of next 4 rows, BO 4 (5, 6, 6, 6, 6) sts.

Work rem 17 (17, 17, 21, 23, 25) neck sts as follows:

## Collar Ribbing

**Row 1:** *K1, p1, rep from * until last st, wyif, sl1 pwise.

**Row 2:** P1, k1, rep from * until last st, wyif, sl1 pwise.

Rep Rows 1 and 2 until collar measures 3½" (8.9cm), BO in ribbing patt.

## Left Front

CO 23 (26, 28, 32, 33, 36) sts.

Work in Broken Rib patt, using the version for odd or even numbers of sts, as appropriate for your size, until the front piece measures the same as the back to the underarm: 15 (15½, 15½, 16, 16, 16½)" (38.1 [39.4, 39.4, 40.6, 40.6, 41.9] cm). End with WS row.

## Shape Armhole

Maintain Broken Rib patt as established throughout shaping of armhole and shoulder.

At beg of next RS row, BO 3 (3, 3, 3, 4, 4) sts.

For all sizes, at beg of next RS row, BO 2 sts.

Dec 1 st at beginning of every RS row 1 (2, 2, 3, 3, 5) times; 17 (19, 21, 24, 24, 25) sts rem.

Continue working even until armhole measures the same length as the back to the beginning of the shoulder shaping: 7½ (8½, 9, 9¼, 9¾, 10)" (19.1 [21.6, 22.9, 23.5, 24.8, 25.4]cm).

## Shape Left Shoulder

Work shoulder shaping on same side as armhole.

Rep Rows 1 and 2 until collar measures
3½" (8.9cm), BO in ribbing patt.

### Right Front

Work right front as for left front, with shaping reversed. The final row before armhole shaping will be a RS row, and the
armhole bind-offs will be on WS rows.

### Sleeves (Make Two)

CO 28 (30, 32, 34, 34. 34) sts. Work k1, p1
ribbing for 2½" (6.4cm).

Start Broken Rib patt, using the version for
an even number of sts and maintaining
pattern as established while increasing 1
st at beg and end of row every 8 (6, 6, 6,
6, 6) rows 6 (7, 7, 7, 9, 10) times. There
will be a total of 40 (44, 46, 48, 52, 54)
sts on needle.

Continue in patt until sleeve measures 16
(16¾, 17½, 18¼, 18¾, 19)" (40.5 [42.6,
44.5, 46.4, 47.6, 48.3]cm).

### Shape Sleeve Cap and Saddle

Maintain Broken Rib patt as established
while shaping Saddle Sleeve Cap and
Saddle.

At beg of next 2 rows, BO 3 (3, 3, 3, 4, 5) sts.

For all sizes, at beg of next 2 rows, BO 2
sts, for a total of 30 (34, 36, 38, 40, 40)
sts on needle.

Dec 1 st at beg and end of row every 4
rows 1 (1, 1, 3, 3, 3) times.

Dec 1 st at beg and end of row every 2
rows 6 (7, 7, 4, 4, 3) times.

BO 2 sts at beg of next 4 (4, 6, 8, 8, 8) rows;
8 (10, 8, 8, 8, 10, 12) sts rem.

Continue in patt on rem sts until saddle
strip measures 3½ (4¼, 5, 5, 5, 5)"
(8.9 [10.8, 12.7, 12.7, 12.7, 12.7]cm).

At beg of row, BO 4 (5, 6, 6, 6, 6) sts.

Work 1 row in Broken Rib patt.

At beg of next row, BO at shoulder 4 (5, 6,
7, 7, 6) sts.

Work the rem 9 (9, 9, 11, 11, 13) neck sts as
follows for collar ribbing.

### Collar Ribbing

**Row 1:** *K1, p1, rep from * until last st, wyif,
sl1 pwise.

**Row 2:** *P1, rep from *k1 until last st, wyif,
sl1 pwise.

## Collar Ribbing

Work k1, p1 ribbing for 3½" (8.9cm). BO in ribbing.

## Finishing

Weave in ends.

With a tapestry needle and matching yarn, sew the side seams and underarm seams. Avoid bulky seams by laying pieces flat and using mattress st to join edges. Stitch sleeves into place by aligning the ribbed saddle section with the collar sections of front and back and sewing in, continuing seams so that armholes match up between sleeves and body. Sew in zipper as follows when sweater is fully assembled:

Pin zipper into place with edges aligned on the WS of the sweater. Leave a small amount of space so that the sweater's sts do not become tangled in the zipper teeth.

With matching thread and needle, attach zipper on WS of left and right fronts with whip st on the outside edge of the zipper. When zipper is attached, take out pins and check alignment of zipper. With a needle and thread, sew a running st seam closer to the teeth of zipper to reinforce it and make sure it is attached to the sweater at all points.

When sweater is completely finished, wet block by washing or dampen the sweater with water. Lay flat to dry.

**note** Do not steam, iron, or otherwise apply heat to the plastic zipper. It will melt.

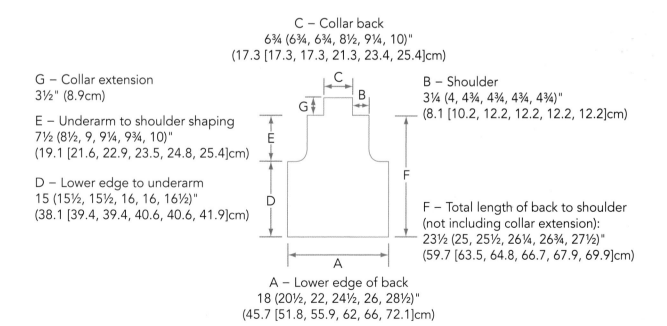

C – Collar back
6¾ (6¾, 6¾, 8½, 9¼, 10)"
(17.3 [17.3, 17.3, 21.3, 23.4, 25.4]cm)

G – Collar extension
3½" (8.9cm)

E – Underarm to shoulder shaping
7½ (8½, 9, 9¼, 9¾, 10)"
(19.1 [21.6, 22.9, 23.5, 24.8, 25.4]cm)

D – Lower edge to underarm
15 (15½, 15½, 16, 16, 16½)"
(38.1 [39.4, 39.4, 40.6, 40.6, 41.9]cm)

B – Shoulder
3¼ (4, 4¾, 4¾, 4¾, 4¾)"
(8.1 [10.2, 12.2, 12.2, 12.2, 12.2]cm)

F – Total length of back to shoulder (not including collar extension):
23½ (25, 25½, 26¼, 26¾, 27½)"
(59.7 [63.5, 64.8, 66.7, 67.9, 69.9]cm)

A – Lower edge of back
18 (20½, 22, 24½, 26, 28½)"
(45.7 [51.8, 55.9, 62, 66, 72.1]cm)

I – Collar front
3½ (3½, 3½, 4½, 4½, 5¼)"
(9.1 [9.1, 9.1, 11.2, 11.2, 13.2]cm)

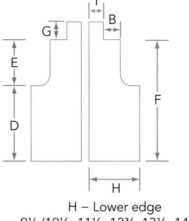

H – Lower edge
9¼ (10½, 11¼, 12¾, 13¼, 14½)"
(23.4 [26.4, 28.4, 32.5, 33.5, 36.6]cm)

L – Width of shoulder strap and collar
3¼ (4, 3¼, 3¼, 4, 4¾)"
(8.1 [10.2, 8.1, 8.1, 10.2, 12.2]cm)

P – Strap plus collar extension
7 (7½, 8¼, 8½, 8½, 8¾)"
(17.8 [19.1, 21, 21.6, 21.6, 22.2]cm)

K – Full sleeve width
20 (22, 23, 24, 26, 27)"
(50.8 [55.9, 58.4, 61, 66, 68.6]cm)

N – Cuff to top of sleeve cap
22 (23¼, 24½, 26¼, 26¾, 26½)"
(55.9 [59.1, 62.2, 66.7, 67.9, 67.3]cm)

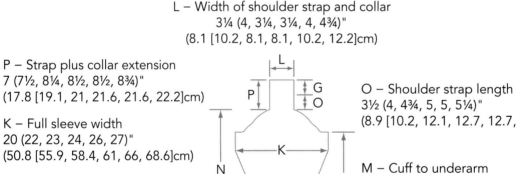

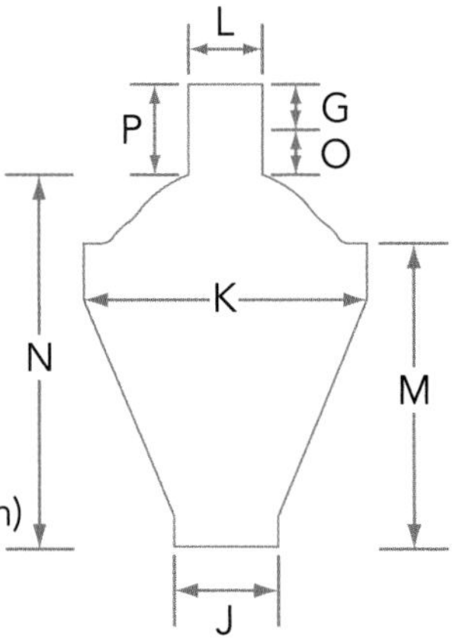

O – Shoulder strap length
3½ (4, 4¾, 5, 5, 5¼)"
(8.9 [10.2, 12.1, 12.7, 12.7, 13.3]cm)

M – Cuff to underarm
16 (16¾, 17½, 18¼, 18¾, 19)"
(40.6 [42.5, 44.5, 46.4, 47.6, 48.3]cm)

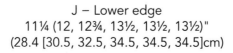

J – Lower edge
11¼ (12, 12¾, 13½, 13½, 13½)"
(28.4 [30.5, 32.5, 34.5, 34.5, 34.5]cm)

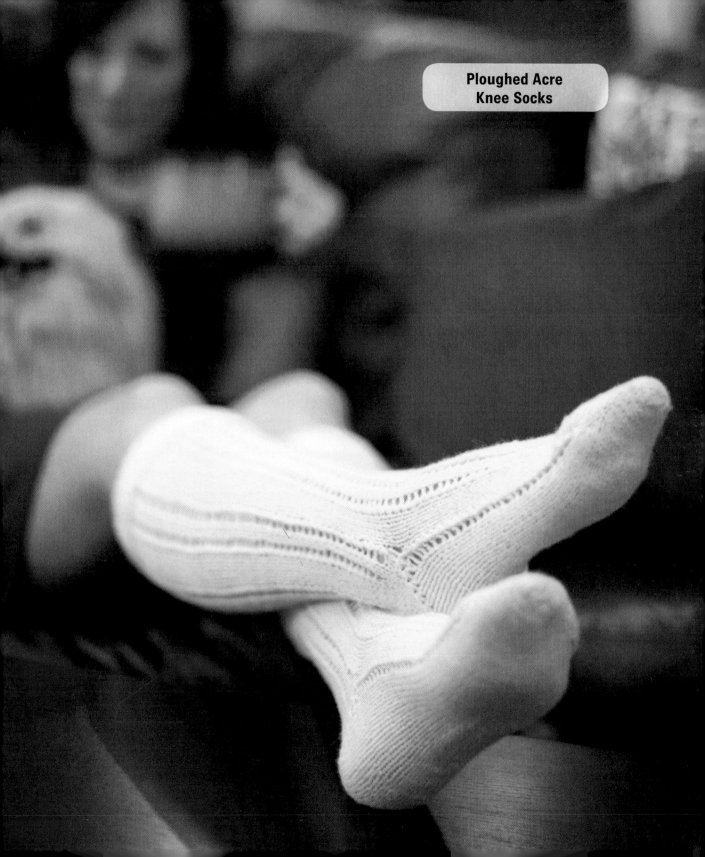

Ploughed Acre
Knee Socks

# Ploughed Acre Knee Socks

This lace pattern is from Barbara Walker's stitch dictionary, *A Treasury of Knitting Patterns* (Charles Scribner's Sons, 1968) and is called "Ploughed Acre." I can think of nothing more beautiful than these twinned rows of crops between the brown earth of a newly planted field, and I wanted it in socks! These toe up, short-row heel socks add a bit of glamour to a practical idea. Knee socks offer an extra layer of warmth in the winter underneath a pair of jeans or a skirt, and with just a little bit of simple lace, socks become, well…sexy, even when the thermostat's turned down.

The pattern allows those who prefer shorter socks that option as well. The yarn I chose for these socks is from Elsa Wool Company, a Cormo sheep ranch in Colorado. The fiber is processed as gently as possible, and the owner, a lifelong farmer, is committed to excellence in everything from sheep care to customer service. If your interest is in supporting natural fibers or U.S. small farms, this is a great yarn to consider. If you live in Colorado or Montana, you're lucky to be able to consider this a local product as the flocks graze in your state.

**Skill Level**
Intermediate

**Finished Measurements**
Sock circumference 8 (9½)" (20.3 [24.1]cm)

Length of sock from toe to heel 9 (10)" (22.9 [25.4]cm) or length to fit recipient

**Size**
Women's Medium (Large)

Length of sock from heel to cuff:

Short option: 10" (25.4cm)

Knee Sock option: 16" (40.6cm) or length to fit recipient

## Materials

**note** If purchasing from Elsa Wool Company for these socks, take care to choose Worsted spun yarn rather than Woolen spun in order to get harder wearing socks that will be less prone to felting.

- 2 skeins of Elsa Wool Company Worsted-Spun 2-ply Sportweight Yarn, 100 percent Cormo wool, 1,360 yd. per lb, 213 yd. (195m), 2.5 oz. (71g), color: White.

or

- 426 yd. (390m) of any sportweight yarn that knits at the same gauge
- U.S. size 1 (2.25mm) double-pointed needles
- U.S. size 2 (2.75mm) double-pointed needles
- Row counter
- 5 stitch markers, 4 of which are split-ring markers or safety pins (to mark rows)
- Tapestry needle

## Gauge

26 sts and 38 rows = 4" (10cm) in stockinette stitch with smaller needles

## Pattern Stitch

### Ploughed Acre Pattern
**Rnd 1:** Knit.
**Rnd 2:** K1, *yo, k2tog, k4, ssk, yo, k2, rep from *, end k1.

## Special Stitch

To form a backward yo, with purl side facing, bring yarn to the back under the needle and then over the top. (The leading side of the loop will be on the back of the needle.) For more information about this technique, see *Simple Socks, Plain and Fancy*, by Priscilla Gibson-Roberts (Nomad Press, 2004).

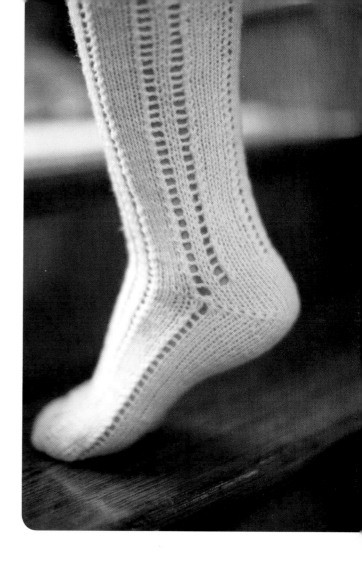

## Instructions
### Make Toe

With #1 (2.25mm) needles, CO 8 sts on 1 dpn.

Inc (kf&b) 1 st in each st and distribute on needles as follows:

4 sts on needle #1, 8 sts on needle #2, 4 sts on needle #3.

Join and pm.

**Rnd 1:** Knit.

**Rnd 2:** Knit until last st of needle #1, inc 1 in that st. On needle #2, k1, inc 1 in next st. Knit until last 2 sts. Inc 1, k1. On needle #3, inc 1, knit to end of rnd.

Rep Rnds 1 and 2 until 52 sts on needles.

### For larger size only:

Rep Rnds 1 and 2 until there are 60 sts on needles.

Work Rnd 1.

Work additional Rnd 2, inc 2 sts only on needle #2 for a total of 62 sts.

### For both sizes:

Redistribute sts on needles as follows:

11 (16) sts on needle #1, 30 (30) sts on needle #2, 11 (16) sts on needle #3.

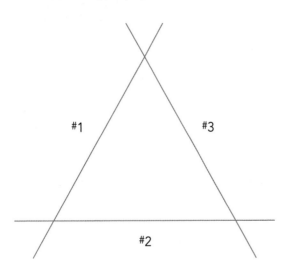

### Begin Pattern

Work Rnd 1 of Ploughed Acre patt as above.

**Rnd 2:** Knit sts on needle #1, work patt as follows on needle #2:

*Yo, k2tog, k4, ssk, yo, k2, rep from *, knit sts on needle #3.

Rep Rnd 1 and 2 until foot measures 7 (8)" (18 [20cm], or 2" (5cm) less than desired length.

End after Rnd 2.

## Work Heel

Redistribute sts as follows, keeping marker at midpoint of heel before first st on needle #1:

13 (15) sts on needle #1, 26 (32) sts on needle #2, and 13 (15) sts on needle #3.

Work the heel over 26 (30) sts, back and forth on needles #1 and #3.

**Row 1 (RS):** On needle #1, k12 (14).

**Row 2 (WS):** Turn work, backward yo, p24 (28), continuing across to needle #3.

**Row 3 (RS):** Turn work, yo, k23 (27).

**Row 4 (WS):** Turn work, backward yo, purl until first paired sts made with a st with yo attached—22 (26) sts purled.

**Row 5 (RS):** Turn work, yo, knit until first paired sts made with yo attached—21 (25) sts knitted.

Rep Rows 4 and 5, with fewer sts worked in St st each time, until 10 (12) sts rem between the yarnovers and you have just completed the following WS row: backward yo, p10 (12) sts.

**Next row:** Turn work, yo, k10 (12), k2tog tbl (yo and next st on needle), closing the gap.

**Next row:** Turn work, backward yo, p11 (13), p2tog (yo and next st on needle), closing the gap.

**Next row:** Turn work yo, knit until reaching 2 yarnovers, k3tog tbl (2 yarnovers and next st on needle).

**Next row:** Turn work, backward yo, purl until reaching 2 yarnovers, p3tog (2 yarnovers and next st on needle).

Rep the last 2 rows, continuing to turn work and dec until all yo pairs have been worked. At the end of the last purl row, p3tog (2 yarnovers and the last st on the needle).

**Next rnd (RS):** Turn work and begin working in the round again. On needle #3, yo, k13 (15), on needle #1, k13 (15), sl yo at end of needle #1 onto needle #2 and k2tog (yo and first st on needle #2), knit across to the last st on needle #2; sl yo on needle #3 onto the end of needle #2 and k2tog (last st on needle #2 and the yo from #3); knit rem 13 (15) sts on needle #3. Sts will be arranged on the needles as follows: #1–13 (15), #2–26 (32), #3–13 (15).

Redistribute sts on the needles as follows so that patt aligns correctly, keeping marker at midpoint of heel before first st. Needle #1 should have 11 (16) sts, needle #2 should have 30 (30) sts, and needle #3 should have 11 (16) sts.

## For large size only:

At beg of rnd, k5. Pm here to indicate beg of Ploughed Acre patt.

## For both sizes:

Work Ploughed Acre patt for leg, beg with Rnd 2 at marker and working around whole sock. When you reach the marker and beg Rnd 1, take care to k1 st (as in the patt instructions) before beginning 10 st rep.

Work for 6" (15cm).

To make shorter socks instead of knee socks, skip the instructions for calf shaping and work ribbing with #1 (2.25mm) needles, as described below.

## Knee Sock Calf Shaping

When leg measures 6" (15cm), switch to larger needles as follows:

Pm to designate length.

Switch one #1 (2.25mm) needle with a #2 (2.75mm) needle. Work 1" (2.25cm) in patt with three #1 (2.25mm) needles and one #2 (2.75mm) needle in the rotation.

*Pm.

Switch another #1 (2.25mm) needle for a #2 (2.75mm) needle. Work 1" (2.25cm) in patt.*

Rep between ** 2 more times, until working with only #2 (2.75mm) needles. At this point, you can remove the markers.

Continue in patt until sock leg (above heel) measures 12" (30.5cm) or desired length.

## Ribbing

Work k2, p2 ribbing for 4" (10cm) or as desired.

BO loosely in patt.

Make second sock for best result!

## Finishing

With a tapestry needle and CO end, carefully close up hole at sock toe. Weave in ends.

Block gently with cool water, avoiding agitation. Lay flat to dry.

# Conclusion:
# Every Little Bit
# Makes a Difference

There are so many choices here, but as you begin to work (in small or big steps) to make a daily difference toward sustainability, your efforts are all valuable. We have so many wonderful options to promote sustainability while we knit. This is a chance to skip the guilt by making a small effort to do things differently. We may not be able to control a lot of aspects of climate change, but through our hobbies, we can choose to make carbon neutral or positive choices—that part is up to us as individuals. You don't have to act on every front at once, and this is an easy place to start.

There are lots of things to consider. Some commit wholly to the concept of sustaining the environment for future generations through biodiversity, sustainable farming practices, and vegan knitting. Others focus on people's immediate needs, while buying for the future. Through those purchases, one can maintain folk and indigenous traditions, support fair trade and fair work conditions, and protect people and the earth from pesticides with organic and natural fibers. There are individuals who decide to concentrate on personal change, reusing their yarn, buying local goods, and changing their habits to conserve resources. Regardless of your choices, the conclusion is simple: every little bit makes a difference.

It's easy to be overwhelmed with all these options when it comes to what is, for most people, an enjoyable leisure time activity. Sure, knitting is important to us, but gosh… what does all this mean for "greening" the rest of our lives? As a person who feels easily overwhelmed by all that is left to be done "to make the world a better place," I can

understand the reaction of those who throw up their hands, claiming that, "as only one person, and only one person's knitting, it can't be that big a deal." However, I'd argue with that response…you can make a difference. I'd start with a different suggestion…a project. Most knitters are thrilled with the prospect of starting a project (right?), this will be fun!

Grab a piece of paper and start to make a list. Go through the table of contents and think about each issue you've read about. What resonates for you? Prioritize what you feel matters and determine which things are not as important for your personal knitting and crochet choices. For each idea you've decided is important, is there one specific thing you'd like to change or commit to doing more consistently? If so, write it down. Write down all the things that occur to you. It might be recycling yarn, supporting more fair trade organizations, searching out fibers that promote biodiversity…the topics are broad and the ideas are endless. I've only covered the tip of the iceberg here, and if we want to

*Making creative use of a former school campus, the Harveyville project is now home to workshops, artists in residence, a small fiber flock, an organic kitchen garden, and laying hens.*

*▶ Hardy sheep on common grazing land in Shetland's Hermaness National Nature Reserve, Scotland.*

keep those icebergs around, we'll all need to keep thinking about the issues and making change.

Put that list in your pocket. Take it out when you start looking at your stash or at your next knitting stitch n' bitch. Talk to your friends about the issues. Tote along your list (along with a list of your needles) when you go to your local yarn store next time. Post it next to your computer if you're prone (as I am!) to online stash shopping adventures.

Every so often, when the list gets crumpled or circumstances change, stop to reconsider your options. Rewrite the list. Discuss it with those friends you know who also think about sustainability. It's okay to change your commitments, especially if there's a new locally grown and produced yarn available, or a brand new charitable foundation associated with a tempting yarn. Give yourself a chance to grow and reconsider your options frequently.

Many encouraging environmental discussions begin with the Chinese philosopher, Lao Tzu's quote, "A journey of a thousand miles begins with a single step." In fact, I like a different translation of his words better. "The journey of a thousand miles begins beneath one's feet." Some interpret this to mean our change doesn't always come from action—that first step—but arises from the stillness, the place where we already are. Knitting often brings about this stillness and this focus. Every stitch is connected to the next. As knitters, we are uniquely situated to understand the connectedness of our world.

We knitters can move toward making a difference while sitting on the couch and knitting for charity or working with a yarn whose purchase helped others! Just as one stitch leads without interruption to the next, so too, can our steps toward a sustainable future. You've already started the journey. We can do it together.

## ✂ *Making a List* ✂

1. Grab a piece of paper (preferably recycled!) and a pen.
2. Open this book to the Table of Contents.
3. Which topics resonate with you? Write those down.
4. Prioritize your choices. What feels most important?

5. For each abstract topic, brainstorm three ways to do something practical that fits into your community and personal knitting routine.
6. Choose one idea to begin.
7. Make it happen!
8. Enjoy your efforts toward more sustainable knitting.
9. Share your experiences with others so they too can make a difference.

# Table of Abbreviations

This table includes the basic knitting and crochet abbreviations used in this book. Some special abbreviations are defined within the patterns.

| Abbreviation | Meaning | Abbreviation | Meaning |
|---|---|---|---|
| ( ) | repeat the instructions in the brackets the specified number of times | p3tog | purl 3 stitches together |
| ** | repeat the instructions between the ** as instructed | patt | pattern |
| beg | beginning | pf&b | purl into front and back of same stitch (increase) |
| BO | bind off | pm | place marker |
| ch | chain (crochet) | psso | pass slipped stitch over |
| cm | centimeter(s) | pwise | purlwise |
| CO | cast on | rem | remaining |
| cont | continue | rep | repeat |
| dec | decrease; decreasing | rnd(s) | round(s) |
| dpn(s) | double-pointed needle(s) | RS | right side |
| est | establish(ed) | sc | single crochet |
| g | Gram(s) | sl | slip |
| inc | increase | sl1 | slip 1 |
| k | knit | sm | slip marker |
| k2tog | knit 2 stitches together | ssk | slip, slip, knit |
| k3tog | knit 3 stitches together | ssp | slip, slip, purl |
| kf&b | knit into front and back of same stitch (increase) | st(s) | stitch(es) |
| kwise | knitwise | St st | stockinette stitch |
| m1tbp | Make 1 through back of purl | tbl | through back loop |
| MC | main color | WS | wrong side |
| mm | millimeter(s) | wyib | with yarn in back |
| oz | ounce(s) | wyif | with yarn in front |
| p | purl | yd(s) | yard(s) |
| p2tog | purl 2 stitches together | yo | yarn over |

# Tips and Techniques

Although *Knit Green* isn't a learn-to-knit book, I want to provide enough information so that beginning to intermediate knitters can successfully make these projects. This section includes instructions for a few of the techniques used in this book. If you need instruction on basic knitting or crochet techniques, check out the many learn-to-knit books on the market, do an Internet search, or support your local yarn store by asking the friendly staff about their classes.

## Knitting

The following knitting techniques are used in projects in this book. If a technique is used in only one project, it is included with the pattern.

### Casting On

In most knitting projects, you can use whatever cast-on technique you prefer. In a few cases, I have suggested a special technique to achieve special results.

#### Backward Loop Cast-On (Also Called Single Cast-On)

1. Start with a slipknot or with a previously established piece of knitting. Wrap the working yarn around your thumb, back to front.
2. Pull working yarn to the back, holding it with your fingers, creating a cross in the yarn between your thumb and fingers.
3. Put needle tip in the loop alongside your thumb. Take your thumb out of the loop and pull on the working yarn to tighten your stitch on the needle.

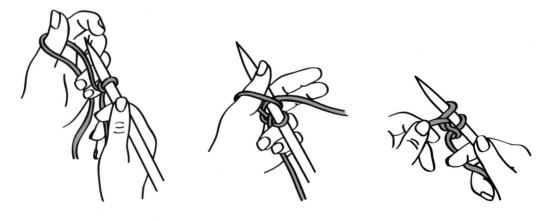

## Long Tail Cast-On (Also Called Double Cast-On)

1. Pull out a "long tail" of yarn about 1" (2.5cm) long for each stitch you need to cast on. Make a slipknot and put it on the needle. This is the first stitch.

2. With the tail of the yarn over your left thumb and the yarn attached to the ball over your index finger, pull the strands open. Grasp the strands in your palm, and pull the needle down to form a V between your thumb and index finger.

3. *Insert the needle into the loop on your thumb, from bottom to top. Bring the needle around the yarn on your index finger from right to left and catch the yarn on the needle. Then pull the yarn back through the loop on your thumb from top to bottom.

4. Pull your thumb out of the loop. You have cast on one more stitch. Reposition your thumb under the tail, and tug gently to tighten the new stitch on the needle. Do not let go of the strands held in your palm.

5. Repeat from * until you have the desired number of stitches.

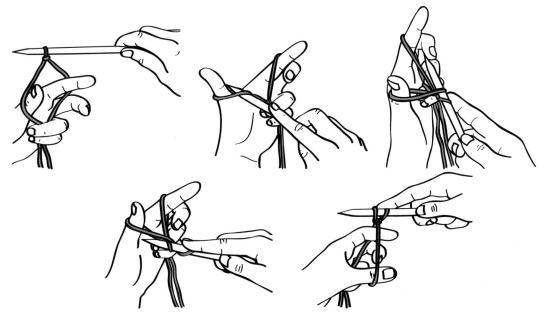

## Eastern/Figure 8 Cast-On

1. Hold two double-pointed needles parallel and wrap yarn in a figure 8 motion around two needles until there are the desired number of loops on each needle.

2. Use your thumb to hold down the yarn tail.

3. With a third double-pointed needles, knit loops from top needle without allowing the bottom needle loops to slide off. Turn work.

4. Knit these loops off second figure 8 needle, knitting through the back loop. You'll now have a small piece of knitting with stitches distributed on two needles.

5. Work according to pattern instructions, introducing third dpn as the stitch count increases.

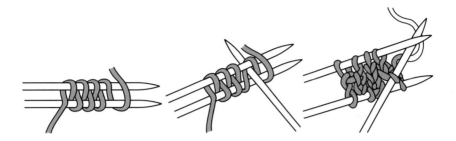

## Binding Off

For the projects in this book you may bind-off using any technique you prefer. If it is not specified, bind-off knitwise on right-side rows and purlwise on WS rows. When a project instructs you to bind-off in pattern, continue working the pattern as established, knitting or purling as you would on a regular row of knitting. After you work each stitch, bind it off in your usual manner.

### Three-Needle Bind-Off

1. Place the two pieces on knitting needles so the right sides of each piece are facing each other with the needles parallel. Both pieces should have the same number of stitches.

2. *Insert a third needle one size larger through the leading edge of the first stitch on each needle. Knit these stitches together as one, leaving 1 stitch on the right-hand needle.

3. Repeat from *, each time slipping the older stitch on the left-hand needle over newer stitch to bind-off.

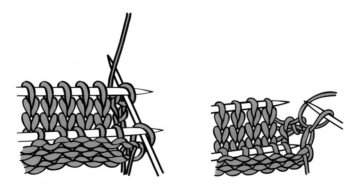

# Special Knitting Techniques

## Make an I-Cord

Cast on stitches onto a single dpn, and knit one row. Slide work to the other end of the needle, pull the yarn across the back of the stitches, and knit into the first stitch. Continue across the row. Repeat for each row, being sure to pull the yarn snugly across the back each time you slide the work across to start a new row (actually a round, but it will feel like a row). This creates a tube shape.

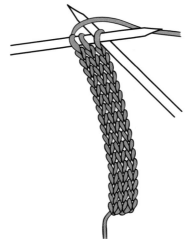

# Sewing Seams

Just as with casting on or binding off, in most knitting patterns you can sew seams using your favorite technique. In a few cases, designers recommend a specific technique for best results on their projects.

## Running Stitch

A running stitch can be used for small seams or for basting pieces together to test the fit. Simply run a tapestry needle with matching yarn up and down through the two pieces of fabric at regularly spaced intervals.

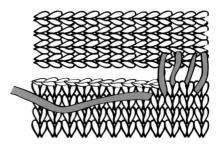

## Whip Stitch

1. With the right sides of the fabric facing up, place the two pieces to be seamed on a flat surface.
2. *With a tapestry needle and matching yarn, use one smooth motion to catch the stitch on the edge of one piece of knitting and then catch a stitch on the other piece. Repeat from * until entire seam is stitched.

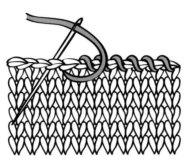

## Mattress Stitch

1. With the right sides facing up, place the two pieces to be seamed on a flat surface.
2. *With a tapestry needle and matching yarn, go under the bar between first and second stitches near the edge of one piece of knitting, then repeat on the other piece.
3. Repeat from *, moving gradually up the sides of the fabric that you are seaming together, until entire seam is stitched, pulling gently to tighten seam after every few stitches.

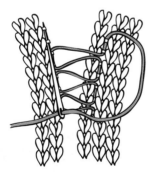
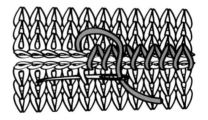

# Blocking

For best results, knitted and crocheted pieces should be blocked after completion. There are several ways to block:

**For garment pieces,** wet the pieces by soaking or spraying with water, form them to the dimensions specified in the pattern, and leave to dry on a towel or blocking board. If desired, pin the pieces in shape until dry. In particular, lace knitting will need to be stretched and pinned to the dimensions specified in the pattern.

**For ribbing or other stretchy pieces,** wash the piece in tepid water and dry flat without stretching or pinning.

**For natural fibers,** some knitters prefer to use steaming as a blocking method. Using a hot iron, gently hold the steaming iron above the pinned-out garment piece. Avoid touching the iron to the fabric itself. This provides a harder block but is slightly more dangerous than the above options because hot steam can cause bad burns. **Note:** Man-made fibers will melt using this process.

**For lace,** soak the piece in tepid water until it is saturated, then stretch it to the dimensions specified in the pattern and pin it in place until dry on a towel or blocking board. Blocking wires can also be use to stretch and block lace. They are available from knitting stores and online retailers, and usually come with instructions.

# Crochet

For knitters who are not familiar with crochet stitches, the following sections should give you enough of a foundation to get started.

## Chain

To begin a crochet piece, you often create a chain of stitches to use as a foundation. Crochet can also be added directly to a piece of knitting.

1. Make a slipknot on your hook. *Bring the yarn over the hook from back to front.
2. Bring the yarn through the loop on your hook. Repeat from * until chain is desired length.

## Single Crochet

1. There will be a loop on the hook to start. Working from right to left: *Insert the hook into the next stitch. Bring the yarn over the hook and pull the working yarn through the loop on the hook. You now have two loops on your hook.
2. Bring the yarn over the hook again and pull the yarn through both loops. One loop remains on the hook. Repeat from * for the desired number of stitches.

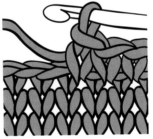

# Resources

A. Feisbusch Corporation
New York, NY
(888) 947-7872
Afeibusch@prodigy.net
www.zipperstop.com

American Livestock Breeds Conservancy
(919) 542-5704
Fax: (919) 545-0022
www.albc-usa.org

American Vegan Society
(856) 694-2887
www.americanvegan.org

Bayeta Classic Sheep and Wool
Connie Taylor
(719) 846-7311
churrosheep@mac.com

Bijou Basin Ranch
P.O. Box 154
Elbert, CO 80106
(303) 601-7544 and (506) 366-5438
Fax: (719) 347-2254
yaks@bijoubasinranch.com
www.bijoubasinranch.com

Blonde Chicken Boutique
www.blondechickenboutique.com

Briggs and Little
York County, NB, Canada
(800) 561-YARN (9276)
Fax: (506) 366-3034
yarninfo@briggsandlittle.com
www.briggsandlittle.com/wool

Centinela Traditional Arts
Chimayo, NM
(877) 351-2180
centinela@newmexico.com
www.chimayoweavers.com

Crystal Palace Yarns/Straw into Gold
Richmond, CA
cpyinfo@straw.com
www.straw.com

Elsa Wool Company
Bayfield, CO
(970) 884-2145
elsa@wool-clothing.com
www.wool-clothing.com

Enchanted Yarns and Fibers (my local
Kentucky yarn store)
Russellville, KY
(270) 772-1675
www.enchantedyarnandfiber.com

Environmental Protection Agency
www.epa.gov

Española Valley Fiber Arts Center
Española, NM
(505) 747-3577
info@evfac.org
www.evfac.org

Euroflax/Louet
Louet North America
Prescott, ON Canada
(800) 897-6444 and (613) 925-4502
info@louet.com
www.louet.com

Frog Tree Yarns
East Dennis, MA
(508) 385-8862
Fax: (508) 385-9476
info@frogtreeyarns.com
www.frogtreeyarns.com

Green Knitter Web site
www.greenknitter.com

Green Mountain Spinnery
Putney, VT
(800) 321-9665 and (802) 387-4528
Fax: (802) 387-4841
spinnery@sover.net
www.spinnery.com

Harris Tweed and Knitwear (This is
only one of the possible ways to
acquire tweed.)
Isle of Harris
United Kingdom
44-0-1859-511114 and
44-0-1859-502040
info@harristweedandknitwear.co.uk
www.harristweedandknitwear.co.uk

The Harveyville Project
13946 Harveyville Road
Harveyville, KS 66431
(785) 589-2714
www.harveyvilleproject.com

Himalaya Yarn (Nettle/Aloo and
Hemp yarn from Nepal)
Colchester, VT
(802) 862-6985
yarn@himalayayarn.com
www.himalayayarn.com

The Jesse B. Collection (Bermuda Bags)
Shillington, PA
(610) 858-6874
customerservice@thejessebcollection.com
www.thejessebcollection.com

Knit Picks
Vancouver, WA
(800) 574-1323
customerservice@knitpicks.com
www.knitpicks.com

Kollage Yarns (Hope-USA Cotton)
Birmingham, AL
(888) 829-7758
info@kollageyarns.com
www.kollageyarns.com

KUSIKUY
P.O. Box 2154
Brattleboro, VT 05303
(802) 254-2273
www.kusikuy.com

Lanaknit Designs Hemp for Knitting
www.lanaknits.com
Nelson, BC Canada
(888) 301-0011
info@lanaknits.com

Lion Brand Yarns
Carlstadt, NJ
(800) 258-YARN (9276)
www.lionbrand.com

Local Harvest
www.localharvest.org

Lopi (U.S. distribution information)
Townsend, MA
(978) 597-8794
www.jcacrafts.com

Lorna's Laces Green Line
Chicago, IL
(773) 935-3803
yarn@lornaslaces.net
www.lornaslaces.net

Mango Moon Yarns
Owosso, MI
(989) 723-5259
info@mangomoonyarns.com
www.mangomoonyarns.com

Mirasol
www.mirasolperu.com

Morehouse Merino Farm
Milan, NY
(866) 470-4852
www.morehousefarm.com

NearSea Naturals (a source for organic stuffing)
Rowe, NM
(877) 573-2913
info@nearseanaturals.com
www.nearseanaturals.com

O-Wool
Middlebury, VT
(802) 388-1313
knit@o-wool.com
www.vtorganicfiber.com/hky.html

Pocket Meadow Farm (a good resource for locally produced and Shetland 2000 yarns)
Berkeley Springs, WV
(304) 258-9702
pocketmeadowfarm@gmail.com
www.pocketmeadowfarm.net

Rare Breeds Survival Trust
Warwickshire, UK
024-7669-6551
Fax: 024-7669-6706
www.rbst.org.uk

Sheep Shop Yarn Company
East Greenwich, RI
(401) 398-7656
sales@SheepShopYarn.com
sheepshopyarn.com

Shokay
(315) 849-3319
info@shokay.com
www.shokay.com

Silk Resource
www.wormspit.com

Stansborough Fibres
Cheryl and Barry Eldridge
Stansborough Limited
Wellington, New Zealand
64-4-566-5591
Fax: 64-4-566-5592
online.enquiries@stansborough.co.nz
www.stansborough.co.nz/sb/ourStory.cfm

Sustainable Table
www.sustainabletable.org

Tierra Wools
Los Ojos Handweavers, LLC
Los Ojos, NM
(888) 709-0979 and (505) 588-7231
Fax: (505) 588-7044
tierrawools@zianet.com

United States Department of Agriculture
(USDA)
www.usda.gov

The United States National Organic Program
www.ams.usda.gov/nop

The Vegan Society
www.vegansociety.com

Yarns International- Shetland 2000 yarn
Cabin John, M.D.
(800) 927-6728 and (301) 229-4203
Fax: (301) 229-4204
info@yarnsinternational.com
www.yarnsinternational.com

## For further reading on textiles and the environment:

Fletcher, Kate. *Sustainable Fashion & Textiles: Design Journeys.* (Earthscan, 2008).

Von Furstenberg, Diane, Earth Pledge, and Leslie Hoffman. *FutureFashion White Papers.* (Earth Pledge, 2007).

# About the Author

Joanne Seiff is a writer, knitwear designer and educator. She now lives in Winnipeg, Manitoba with her biology professor husband and her two bird dogs, Harry and Sally. Joanne grew up in Virginia and has also lived in upstate New York, Durham, North Carolina, and Bowling Green, Kentucky. In her free time, she enjoys spinning, knitting, cooking, taking long walks with her dogs, reading, and good conversations with friends. Her first book, *Fiber Gathering*, is about U.S. fiber festivals. She writes for a wide variety of online and print publications. See more of her work and knitwear designs on her Web site, www.joanneseiff.com, and read what she's up to on her blog, Yarn Spinner, www.joanneseiff.blogspot.com.

## Additional Photography

Page 4: ©Dr. James Vreeland, Jr.

Page 6: ©Steven Ford

Page 16: ©Carl Koop

Page 18: ©Nikol Lohr

Page 35: ©Stockphoto.com/LyaC

Page 37: ©iStockphoto.com/George Clerk

Page 48: ©Dave Wheeler

Page 51: ©iStockphoto.com/Tommy Martin

Page 61: ©Tamara Stenn

Page 69: ©iStockphoto.com/Virginia Zozaya

Page 85: ©Matthew C. Mole

Page 87: ©iStockphoto.com/Brasil2

Page 106: By Jodi Bratch

Page 108: By Jodi Bratch

Page 109: ©Tara Swiger

Page 120: ©Tara Swiger

Page 122: ©iStockphoto.com/Craig Cozart

Page 134: By Jodi Bratch

Page 136: By Jodi Bratch

Page 150: ©Nikol Lohr

Page 153: ©iStockphoto.com/Lisbeth Landstrøm

Page 163: ©Martin Poppmeier

# Index

## W

washcloth, 83
Waves and Stars: Knitted
   Napkins, 117–119
weaving, New Mexico, 50–52
whip stitch, 159
wood, 38
wool
   organic, 86–88
   sheep breeds, 5
   sustainability and, 22

## Y

yak fiber, 22, 24
yarn shops' disconnect from
   farms, 17
Yarn Spinner blog, 166
Yarns International, 57, 165

## Z

Zafu: A Churro Cushion, 12–15
Zigzag Butterfly Table Runner,
   40–43
zipper, 14